NLP: Principles in Practice

Lisa Wake *is Managing Director of*
Awaken Consulting and Training Services Ltd.

After starting her career in NHS clinical practice as a nurse, Lisa moved into NHS management in 1992, until she left to commence her own shared business in 1997. Using NLP (Neurolinguistic Programming) as a launch pad, Lisa has developed extensive experience as a Coach, Facilitator, Change Agent, Trainer, Supervisor and Mentor. Now a Master Trainer of NLP, Lisa is also accredited by the UKCP as a neurolinguistic psychotherapist and has a MSc in Advanced Clinical Practice focusing on the applied psychology of NLP.

Lisa has served as Chair and Vice Chair of UKCP (United Kingdom Council for Psychotherapy) in a voluntary capacity and was instrumental in working with the Government and Department of Health on the statutory regulation of psychology, psychotherapy and counselling, and the recently published White Paper on the regulation of non-medical professionals. She worked closely with Skills for Health in implementing the ground work for the development of National Occupational Standards for Psychotherapy.

Lisa is advisor to Association of NLP and was also on the steering committee of the first International NLP research conference at University of Surrey. Renowned for her track record of ethics, training and standards in NLP, Lisa is one of the few academically published researchers and writers within the field of NLP. In partnership with Jeremy Lazarus and the Lazarus Consultancy, Lisa runs the world's first UK university approved Trainers Training, and has mapped NLP training against postgraduate educational competencies.

Lisa's recent groundbreaking publication on the applied psychology of NLP is currently being utilised by the US Military to inform the development of a programme for the US Veterans Association.

Lisa is actively involved in Initiatives of Change, a non-government organisation working for peace, reconciliation and human security worldwide, stressing the importance of personal responsibility, ethical leadership and building trust across the world's divides.

Combining an active business consultancy, research and writing career, Lisa balances her working life with an attempt at 'The Good Life' with her husband and business partner, Mark. They keep chickens and grow most of their own produce which is then used to cater for their in-house training programmes.

NLP

Principles in Practice

Lisa Wake

NLP: Principles in Practice
First published in 2010 by;
Ecademy Press
48 St Vincent Drive, St Albans, Herts, AL1 5SJ
info@ecademy-press.com
www.ecademy-press.com

Printed and Bound by; Lightning Source in the UK and USA
Set in Gill Sans and Footlight MT by Karen Gladwell
Cover artwork and illustrations by Michael Inns

Printed on acid-free paper from managed forests. This book is
printed on demand, so no copies will be remaindered or pulped.

ISBN 978-1-905823-78-9

A CIP catalogue record for this book is available from
the British Library.

Contents

Acknowledgements

My thanks are offered to Ed Luttrell, Franca Mongiardi and Mark Wake, all of whom have given me their feedback, suggestions and comments on the content of this book.

I also acknowledge students and learners of NLP who have joined me on this journey of discovery and have aided me in structuring my thinking as the book has developed.

I am indebted to many in the NLP field, not least Richard Bandler and John Grinder as the co-creators of NLP along with the others who have either influenced me through my reading or who have supported me on the path of discovery in my learning. I apologise for any omissions.

Gregory Bateson	*Shelle Rose Charvet*
Robert Dilts	*Milton Erickson*
Charles Faulkner	*Steve Gilligan*
Tad James	*Sue Knight*
Judith DeLozier	*Jane Mathison*
Bill O'Hanlon	*Fritz Perls*
Ernest Rossi	*Virginia Satir*
Dave Shephard	*Susi Strang-Wood*
Paul Tosey	*Paul Watzlawick*
Wyatt Woodsmall	*Jeff Zeig*

Chapter One

Introduction

NLP as an approach

THE PURPOSE of this book is to provide an understanding of NLP for the reader and includes evidence of the tools, techniques and methodology where this is available. The book is designed to be read by a wide range of audiences. It provides a good grounding for individuals who want to study NLP further. It is also for individuals who want to underpin their existing knowledge with an evidence base for the approach and to understand how the various components of NLP can be applied across a range of contexts.

NLP (Neuro-Linguistic Programming) is beginning to develop an increasing evidence base that both challenges and supports its approach as an applied psychology. This book includes the current evidence base as it appears in 2010 and it should be noted that the evidence within this book is a simplistic review of the existing material. The only references that have been critically reviewed are those relevant to the study of NLP as a psychotherapy. All other evidenced papers are taken from abstracts and the rigour of the studies has not been critically appraised. This not withstanding there is considerably more evidence available than is accessible by the general public and I hope that the publication of the recent Current Research in NLP Volume I will be the first step in developing this more substantive evidence base.

The expanding evidence base and credibility of NLP is assisting the accessibility to and spread of NLP across a number of different disciplines. Currently in 2010 there are a number of Universities offering undergraduate, postgraduate and doctorate programmes that include NLP either wholly or partially. Large organisations in the public and commercial sectors have adopted the principles and practices of NLP. There has also been a considerable shift since

2000 in the teaching of NLP within management processes as a mainstream topic rather than camouflaged as something else. NLP has also been adapted and integrated into psychotherapy practice and is now a mainstream psychotherapy recognised by the UK Council for Psychotherapy (UKCP). Educational programmes are littered with some of the tools and techniques of NLP with NLP being integrated from Government policy level down to grass roots.

Book overview

This book covers the main tools and techniques of NLP. Apart from this first chapter, each chapter follows the same layout. The overview and rationale for each tool/technique or philosophy is given. A literature review has been undertaken and any relevant literature to support or challenge the model is included. Any concepts that are directly related to the subject matter are summarised as are the principles of why the particular technique works and how it links back to the overarching theory and principles of NLP. How the technique works is then described followed by the key steps involved in applying the technique. Each section then concludes with a recommended exercise to follow and examples of how the technique can be applied across a number of different contexts.

This first chapter summarises NLP as an approach and briefly covers some background information on the three therapists modelled by Bandler and Grinder, Virginia Satir, Fritz Perls and Milton Erickson.

Chapter 2 provides a comprehensive review of the history of NLP from two perspectives. The first perspective is the standard map of NLP which has been amended and updated. The second perspective is the influences on the map of NLP taking into account the influences on Satir, Perls, Erickson and Bateson.

Chapter 3 begins with the outcome oriented nature of NLP and includes the relationship of NLP to other goal oriented processes. There is a comprehensive evidence base to support the use of goal setting, and a critique of the potentially negative impacts of goal setting activities.

Chapter 4 reviews the techniques that are at the heart of beginning to understand other people.

Chapter 5 builds on the understanding developed in chapter 4 and looks at some of the processes that enable you to view things from alternative perspectives. This includes processes that are effective at developing creative thinking. Some of the steps to working with mediation processes are discussed as well as enabling an alternative viewpoint using language processes such as metaphor utilisation and reframing.

Chapter 6 is the first chapter that looks at some of the change processes that are available within NLP. Processes that enable us to change how we think are covered in detail as are processes that enable us to understand and change decision making and motivation patterns. The chapter also looks at how we can change our response in situations where our feelings override our thoughts and we go into an unuseful state or feeling.

Chapter 7 addresses change management theory within NLP and provides an effective model that enables change within a given system. The same model can be used as a coaching tool or to diagnose where organisations or individuals may be experiencing challenges.

Chapter 8 provides a comprehensive review of the language techniques of NLP and how these can be applied in a number of contexts.

Chapter 9 builds on the language of the previous chapter and includes a process for meeting the learning and decision making needs of a diverse audience. The process included within this chapter provides a template for presentations in any context.

Chapter 10 looks at motivational influences and drives. Values are the core elements of our personality that enable us to make decisions and motivate ourselves. A background is given on how values are formed and the influences that effect the development of values. This is then continued into an understanding of the personality traits that drive our behaviour in a given context.

Chapter 11 provides the final piece for NLP and is the basis for the development of all NLP techniques. Modelling is described at process level and NLP is discussed in the context of other modelling approaches.

Chapter 12 concludes this book with a review of NLP as it has developed in a number of contexts, further learning and suggested ways forward for NLP and a list of reference sources that can be accessed to further your understanding.

Background to NLP

NLP is based on behaviourist principles and was developed by the co-founders John Grinder and Richard Bandler in 1976. Initially defined as the 'Study of the

Structure of Subjective Experience' it has gone on to develop many definitions and interpretations, discussed in chapter 2.

NLP was developed through modelling the behaviours of a number of different experts from fields as diverse as systems theory, linguistics, psychotherapy, education and artificial intelligence. As a behavioural methodology NLP is:

- ❧ An Epistemology – a philosophy that deals with knowledge, especially with regard to its method, validity and scope (Oxford English Dictionary)

- ❧ A Methodology – the processes and procedures for applying knowledge and values

- ❧ A Technology – tools that assist the application of the knowledge and values.

The three therapists

Virginia Satir

Virginia Satir was the co-founder of family therapy in the United States, starting her therapy career with alcoholics and the homeless, and it was from this work that she developed an interest in family therapy. She operated from a systemic perspective and set up the Mental Research Institute in Palo Alto, California, working with Gregory Bateson. As an advocate of systems therapy, her work often involved changing either the structure of the system or the functions of individuals within the system. She did this by using alternative perspectives to enable people to view their experiences differently. Satir would consider the roles within the families that she worked with and how, by changing these, the family system would then change. She would encourage her clients to negotiate with the more destructive imprinted aspects of their personality to enable the development of healthier functioning. Bandler's modeling of her linguistic patterns formed the Meta Model language patterns of NLP which enabled the challenging of unuseful perceptions of self in relation to others. Satir's writings: Peoplemaking (1972) and Changing with Families (Bandler, Grinder and Satir 1976).

Fritz Perls

Originally trained as a Freudian psychoanalyst, Perls' increasing interest in phenomenology: the study of consciousness and the objects of direct experience, and existentialism (the existence of a person as a free and responsible agent) led to his development of Gestalt therapy. His book, Ego, Hunger and Aggression

(1969) set the stage for Gestalt therapy as a discipline. Perls' perspective in therapy recognised that individuals are constantly developing and will devise behaviours that are continually self organising and self actualising. He also believed that people do not need fixing, that the solution already exists within the client and it is just a matter of enabling them to access this. Perls was one of the first therapists that utilised sensory processing in his communication with clients, including the use of sight, sound, touch and feelings as part of his therapy. Bandler's very early work that influenced the development of NLP was based on his modelling of Perls. Bandler studied much of Perls' linguistic patterns through papers that he had written as well as some video recordings of his case material.

Milton Erickson

Erickson first began his career as a medical doctor and a Masters graduate in psychology. He started to practise hypnosis in the 1920s and worked as a psychiatrist in the 1930s in Massachusetts. He developed a particular interest in the use of hypnosis in a therapy setting and spent much of his time researching and teaching therapeutic hypnosis, as well as working from a private practice in Phoenix, Arizona. Although initially considered a controversial figure his work in the latter years of his life achieved considerable recognition.

Erickson had suffered from poliomyelitis as a young man and had learnt much of what later came to influence his work during his recovery from this illness. Through his illness he developed astute observation skills and was able to quickly recognise contradictions between people's verbal and non verbal patterns of behaviour.

Bandler and Grinder (1975) identified Erickson as an expert at working with the subjective experience of a client. They modelled the linguistic patterns of Erickson and also his observational skills.

Much of Erickson's work has been portrayed in his collection of seminars and papers (1985) and his co-authored works with Ernest Rossi (1976, 1989).

Chapter Two

History and the Map of NLP

From the very beginning

NLP EVOLVED through the work of an interdisciplinary community who had a common curiosity around communication, change and influence (DeLozier 1985). Out of this emerged the patterns that later became known as NLP. NLP was developed in the mid 1970's by Richard Bandler, a student of mathematics, and John Grinder, a professor of linguistics. NLP is a behavioural model that consists of a series of tools and techniques modelled on performance excellence. Bandler and Grinder's original modelling was of Virginia Satir, the founder of family therapy in the US and Fritz Perls, the father of gestalt therapy. The results of this modelling were published in *Structure of Magic I* and *II* (1975, 1976). Bandler and Grinder's subsequent modelling of Milton Erickson, MD and Hypnotherapist, published in *Patterns of the Hypnotic Techniques of Milton Erickson, Vols I* and *II* (1975, 1977) contributed further to the body of knowledge. Another important influence in Bandler and Grinder's work has been the British Anthropologist, Gregory Bateson (1972) who worked with the Palo Alto group.

Although NLP was first used in the world of therapy it soon developed application in other fields. The outstanding results that NLP claims to achieve have led to the approach being incorporated into areas such as leadership, team working, selling, training and development, sports coaching, customer service and health care.

Following the early work by Bandler and Grinder much has been added to the field of NLP and I have presented two maps. The first map is the body of knowledge as it has been developed since its initial creation as a model **- see table 1**. The second map of NLP is viewed from the wider psychological map that in many ways has influenced the work of Satir, Perls and Erickson as well as Bandler and Grinder **- see table 2**. It is worth noting that there are parallels to a range of psychological approaches that are well respected models within their field.

Map of the History of NLP

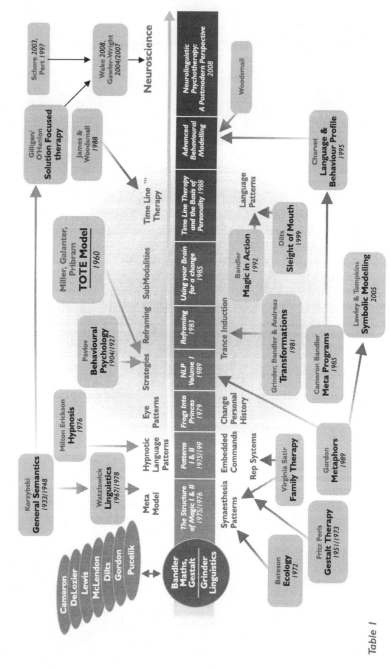

Table 1

Map of the Influences on NLP

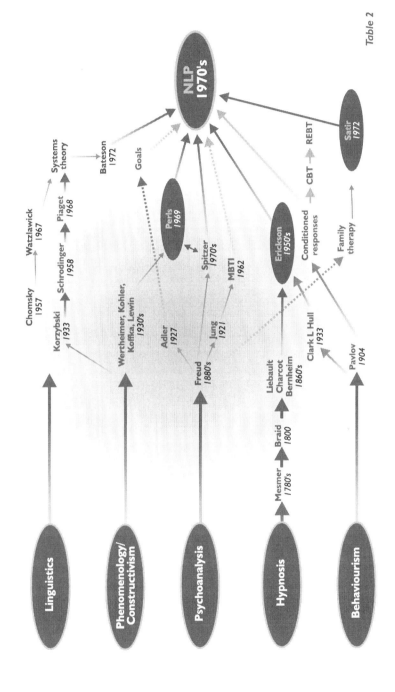

Table 2

The NLP Communication Model

Diagram 1 - The Model

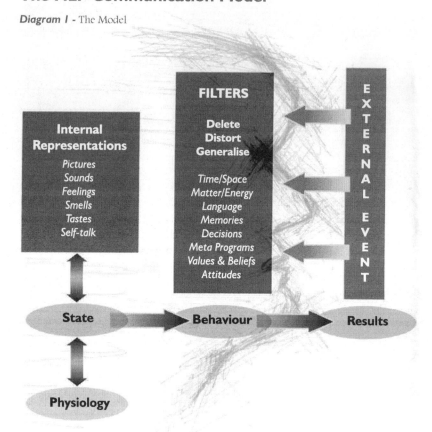

Rationale for the model

The model of communication that is traditionally taught in NLP assumes that we experience the world through a set of filters which cause us to delete, distort and generalise information to be able to make sense of it. Tosey and Mathison (2009) comment that this map, although seen to be representing Bandler and Grinder's work on perceptual filters, only emerged in James and Woodsmall's 'Timeline Therapy' in 1988. Deletions, distortions and generalisations occur as a result of our life experiences. For example if we have a memory of always failing at examinations, we may enter the next examination generalising on our past experience, deleting information that may enable us to pass the examination and possibly even distorting questions into something that we can't answer. Our internal state will most likely be negative, which will directly affect our physiology, behaviour and therefore our results. If we have a memory of always succeeding at examinations, we are likely to do the opposite, filter positively, maintain a positive state and create a positive result. Within this filtering process, it is said that we 'manage' our internal representations down to 7 ± 2 chunks of information that we can handle or process consciously. The remainder of the information is processed unconsciously.

Underpinning and associated theories

There are a number of underpinning theories within linguistics, cybernetics, psychology, and human development that all provide a model of communication based on perceptual filters.

Cybernetics – Anthropologist Gregory Bateson was of great influence in the development of NLP particularly in its early days. He developed the work of Wiener (1948) who was the first person to identify the feedback principle, that all life forms change their actions in response to their environment. Bateson (1972/2000) suggested that within communication the only thing that is relevant are the messages received including the relationship between messages and gaps in messages and it is the 'perception of an event that is real' (p. 250). The message that is received is at a neurophysiologic level and is only relevant in context as the self only exists in relation to the syntax of our experiences. This underpins the NLP presupposition that 'all meaning is context dependent'.

Linguistic and Communications Theory was first introduced to NLP from Korzybski's work, 'Science and Sanity' (1933) and added to by the linguistic theories of Chomsky (1957) and Watzlawick (1978). These models assume that all information held within the somatic (felt body sense) and linguistic reality of an individual is based on the results of the filtering processes of the receiver and is entirely subjective. Watzlawick (1978) expanded on the subjective nature of experience by considering the roles of the different cerebral hemispheres. The left hemisphere utilises logic, semantics and phonetics to create a version of reality that is based on data and providing verbal reasoning. Whereas right hemispheric processing is concerned with pattern recognition, relationships, perceptions of gestalts and abstract thinking. Watzlawick proposes that the right hemisphere is more attuned to the primary senses and the left hemisphere to secondary processing and considers the relationship between thinking and feeling, and perception and intuition, relating this back to Jungian typology (p. 16).

There are also similarities to Shannon & Weaver's communication theory which proposed a mathematical theory of communication, and was initially used to gain greater capacity in communication within the Bell Telephone Company. Weaver applied this theory to interpersonal communication and it has become well known as a model of communication.

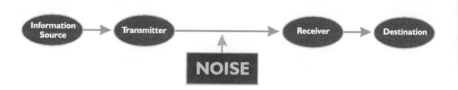

Diagram 2 – Shannon and Weaver's Model of Communication (1949)

Developmental Theory – Although not core to NLP and certainly ignored by the main early developers, Dilts (2000), identified early attachment relationships as being key to forming a sense of self. He referred to Lorenz's (1935/1970) imprinting theory as a way of understanding the subjective nature of our personality and how this develops through time and informs our sense of reality. Within NLP the sense of self is based purely on the subjective experience of the client, theories of which abound in psychoanalytic literature. Klein's (1932) work on Object Relations identified that the sense of self emerged from the processing of social cognitions and our affective response to relationships. Bowlby (1969), in his work on attachment theory, identified the primacy of the need for a relationship as a way of developing a sense of self. He argued that the sense of self is developed predominantly within this relational structure, i.e., the client can only gain a sense of self as they view themselves in relation to the other, which can include any objects that they have an emotional response to. Bowlby (1969, 1980) describes this pattern of behavioural and belief representations or filters as a series of mental representations of the self and others and self interactions, and that this combination leads to the acquisition of dependent traits and behavioural responses.

Stern (1985) has identified that individuals gain a greater sense of self over time, which is formulated according to the quality of interpersonal interactions. These then become generalised over time resulting in the infant developing generalised behavioural traits.

Gerhardt's (2004) work on infant development and communication provides an excellent overview of the neurolinguistic and somatic reality of the developing infant. The early development of an infant is purely reactive to his environment. As the neuro-physiological structures of the infant develop, the infant begins to make meaning of his experience, which then become generalised reactions over time. These reactions are maintained at a very basic functional level and begin to inform the expectations and filters that the child and later the adult has.

Evidence base

There is an evidence base for the concept of processing 7 ± 2 'bits' of information which is based in Miller's (1956) theory of the amount of information that can be held in short term memory processing. The figure is based on the ability to process 'chunks' of information before performance is reduced and varies according to each individual and also the information being processed. Murata et al (2001) were able to replicate this study in reviewing memory processing ability in syntactic structure. Cowan (2001) also supported the view that memory is sorted into manageable chunks of information and that on average, individuals will sort information into 3 or 4 manageable chunks.

Definitions

There are a number of definitions of NLP from the very short to the very long.

Dilts, Grinder, Bandler, DeLozier (1980)

The study of the structure of subjective experience.

Joseph O'Connor & John Seymour (1990 p. 1)

'NLP is the art and science of personal excellence. Art because everyone brings their unique personality and style to what they do, and this can never be captured in words or techniques. Science because there is a method and process for discovering the patterns used by outstanding individuals in any field to achieve outstanding results.'

Joseph O'Connor (2001 p. 2)

- ❧ NLP is the study of the structure of subjective experience
- ❧ NLP is an accelerated learning strategy for the detection and utilization of patterns in the world (John Grinder)
- ❧ NLP is the epistemology of returning to what we have lost – a state of grace (John Grinder)
- ❧ NLP is an attitude and a methodology that leaves behind a trail of techniques (Richard Bandler)
- ❧ NLP is the influence of language on our mind and subsequent behaviour
- ❧ NLP is the systemic study of human communication (Alex Von Uhde)
- ❧ NLP is the method for modelling excellence so it can be duplicated.

As we move into the different applications of NLP there are again a number of different definitions:

Education

Richard Churches (2007) has made a substantial contribution to NLP within the field of education and he defines NLP as a model of studying excellence. 'NLP is not only what effective people do but also how they go about doing it. This includes the visible external behaviours/language of highly effective people, the internal mental processes that they use and the way in which they think. (2007 p. 1).

Health

Lewis Walker, General Practitioner, describes NLP as 'a behavioural technology which not only can really help patients to change quickly, it is also easy to learn and apply in any medical consultation'. He goes on to say, 'NLP is mainly an attitude of mind which has given birth to many techniques which obtain results in the real world. It is an attitude of intense curiosity about people. It involves getting curious about the structure of their internal world and how it manifests in behaviours – some of which may lead to problems, others lead to solutions. By modelling people who obtain exceptional results with patients – whether those people are doctors, nurses, psychologists, therapists, counsellors, etc. – and finding out how they do what they do, NLP has opened the door for all those interested in gaining these skills to acquire them rapidly.' (2004 p. 5).

In alcoholic addictions work, Sterman (1990 p. 13) defines NLP as 'an artful technology for studying the structure of subjective experience and the limitations these subjective experiences impose on each individual. With as much precision and reliability as is available to this young field today, NLP has developed methods, skills, and strategies for increasing and expanding these internal representations of human beings to allow for the construction of an effective repertoire of internally generated choices in people's multitudinous life situations.'

Management

Tosey and Mathison (2009 p. 13), in their critical appreciation of NLP for managers, consider the six faces of NLP.

'Practice: *NLP as a behaviour, or practical communication – what people do;*

Philosophy: *NLP as a body of ideas and principles;*

Product: *NLP as a commodity that can be consumed.'*

Sports

Former semi-professional footballer Lazarus describes NLP as 'the new science of success, a series of techniques and processes to help you to use the language of your mind (that's the 'Neuro Linguistic' element) to program yourself for success. At its core, a main aspect of what NLP is about is how to control your mind (and to help others to do the same) and therefore influence the results you get.' (2006).

Therapy

McDermott and Jago (2001) define neurolinguistic psychotherapy as 'a therapy of what is possible; it opens for the client and therapist a voyage which is genuinely into the unknown' (p. 11).

Kostere and Malatesta (1990) refer to neurolinguistic psychotherapy as a model that facilitates choice for the client by assisting clients to change the 'limits in their model of the world' (p. 20). They view the purpose of therapy as 'working with clients in order to facilitate the expansion of their world model, that is, to open new possibilities, to broaden the scope and depth of their world views, and to expand their models' (p. 20).

The European Association for Neurolinguistic Psychotherapy (EANLPt) (2010) define neurolinguistic psychotherapy as 'a systemic imaginative method of psychotherapy with an integrative-cognitive approach. The principal idea of Neurolinguistic Psychotherapy (NLPt) is the goal-orientated work with a person paying particular regard to his/her representation systems, metaphors and relation matrices. In the course of the therapeutic work in NLPt the verbal and analogue shaping and the integration of the expressions of one's life and digital information processes is given an equal share of attention. The aim of the method consists in accompanying and giving support to human beings so that they can obtain ecologically compatible goals. Further the method helps to position the subjectively good intentions underlying the symptoms of illness and/ or dysfunction so that old fixations about inner and outer unproductive behaviour and beliefs can be dissociated and new subjectively and intersubjectively sound behaviours and beliefs can be established and integrated.'

The Neurolinguistic Psychotherapy and Counselling Association (NLPtCA) (2010) defines neurolinguistic psychotherapy as 'a specialised form of Neuro Linguistic Programming (NLP). The idea is that we work from and react to the world as we construct it from our experiences rather than directly from the "real world". We build our own unique models or maps of the world. Although all such maps are genuine to each of us, no one map is fully able to represent the "real world". Further, NLP is a way of exploring how people think, identifying success and then applying these successful actions or even beliefs in ways that work. This has proved practical and effective in a wide range of applications and situations. Using this form of what is called "modelling" change can be quite quick. NLPt is broad based and draws on concepts from many areas of psychology and psychotherapy. Influences stem from the Gestalt 'school', the family therapy of Virginia Satir, Ericksonian brief therapy, and humanistic psychology. There are also clear links with the fields of systems theory, behavioural psychology and linguistics.'

Presuppositions of NLP

Underpinning NLP is a series of assumptions or presuppositions that, if adopted in communicating with others, can facilitate a more effective interaction. These presuppositions have been developed from an understanding of the beliefs of the three therapists who were originally modelled i.e. Erickson, Perls and Satir. In reading books on NLP there are many variations on the presuppositions and I have included a summary of them as they are portrayed by Dilts (2002 p. 1001–1002).

1 The 'map' is not the 'territory' – people respond to their own perceptions of reality.

Each of us has a subjective map of our reality in the 'here and now' and the behaviour that we show to the world is our map, based on precisely how we are filtering our experience. The territory is the deep structure of our experience and includes our past experiences, our behavioural choices in other contexts and our neurological and linguistic make up. An example of the map and the territory can be considered in the context of the response when required to sit an exam as outlined earlier. The person who demonstrates a fear of exams may present this as their map; however their territory may consist of an infinite number of variables for the cause of the fear, e.g. the last time they sat an exam they got stung by a wasp, rather than a series of failures in examinations. They may fear exams but may not fear practical assessments such as driving tests or clinical examinations such as eye tests. This provides the potential to access resources that exist within the territory to enable a change in the presenting map, recognising that people are always much more than their behaviours.

2 The meaning of a communication to another person is the response it elicits in that person, regardless of the intent of the communicator

or

The meaning of communication is the response you get.

We hold 100% responsibility for our communication in the same way that the person we are communicating with holds 100% responsibility for their communication. The meaning that the person on the receiving end of the communication infers from our communication becomes the meaning of the communication, whether we chose to communicate this or not. This gives us choice in how we communicate to others, if our communication is misread or does not elicit the desired response we can then choose to communicate differently to elicit a different and more preferred response.

3 No response, experience, behaviour is meaningful outside of the context in which it was established, or the response it elicits next

or

All meaning is context dependent.

It is possible to make meaning of anything that we observe and if we take the behaviour out of context it can give it an entirely different meaning. A common example that is used is 'whispering'. A child whispering to a parent will have a different meaning to a group of doctors whispering at the end of a patient's bed or a whisper between two lovers. Yet the behaviour is the same. By changing the context of behaviour we can change its meaning which gives us an opportunity to literally reframe an experience. This is discussed further in chapter 5.

4 Mind-and-body form a cybernetic system.

This presupposition is based in the theories of neuroscience and considers that there is a direct link between the mind and the body. Our thoughts impact on our body and vice versa. For example if we are feeling low about something and then we move our eyes up and to the right we can literally change our feeling in an instance. This is explained further in Eye Patterns in chapter 4. We can also use processes such as visualisation to enhance our performance, Lazarus (2006) provides some good examples of how this can be used in enhancing sports performance. Pert's (1997) studies into neuroscience and the immune system have coined the phrase 'psychoneuroimmunology' which has demonstrated that our internal dialogue can literally influence how our neurology and immunology work. Erickson, one of the therapists who influenced the modellers Bandler and Grinder, would utilise the mind-body system to communicate with one component of a person's physiological or emotional make up to directly influence another aspect. Evidence of this is seen in his work in 'My voice will go with you, the teaching tales of Milton Erickson.' (Rosen 1992). Chopra (1989) has also brought the principles of Ayurvedic medicine into NLP and has introduced three concepts on the mind-body system.

1. That intelligence is present everywhere in our bodies
2. That our own inner intelligence is superior to any that we try to substitute from outside
3. That intelligence is more important than the matter of the body, as without the intelligence the body would be redundant.

5 **The processes that take place within a person and between people and their environment are systemic. Our bodies, our societies and our universe form an ecology of systems and subsystems all of which interact with and mutually influence each other and a pattern of associations (anchors) may be set up through a single trial experience in contrast to linear repetitions.**

This presupposition links to the previous one of the mind and body being a cybernetic system and brings in the additional theories that underpin the process of anchoring or triggered responses that is taught in NLP. Anchoring comes from the theory of operant conditioning (Skinner 1961) which is covered in detail in chapter 6. All behaviour is generated via a cause/effect system of either positive or negative reinforcement and is the basis of behaviour modification programmes such as Cognitive Behaviour Therapy (CBT) and motivational interviewing. Any behaviours that result in a reward response will automatically be repeated to see if the same reward can be elicited, e.g. if someone gets positive attention every time they become ill, they will set up a response to generate a heightened feeling of being unwell to gain attention. If someone experiences pain or emotionally difficult feelings in response to a behaviour, this will reduce the chance of the behaviour being replicated. This process is occasionally included in NLP based sales trainings. I know of trainers who set up painful stimuli in response to poor sales responses e.g. if a sales person does a particular behaviour that is thought to be negative he is encouraged to pluck a tight rubber band on his wrist to cause pain, so that the next time he starts to repeat the unuseful behaviour he will be reminded of the pain that was generated last time. There is the potential however, that if this serves some kind of secondary gain or benefit for the sales person he may prefer to do more of this negative behaviour as he gets a perceived reward from it. I discuss how this process can be used more ecologically in a case study in my book on Neurolinguistic Psychotherapy (2008), pages 27 – 28.

6 **We respect each person's model of the world – No individual map is any more 'real' or 'true' than any other. All maps have some validity**
or
Respect for the client's model of the world.

Linking back to the notion that 'the map is not the territory' this presupposition requires us to respect maps of the world as each one is valid in the experience of the individual. By understanding the 'map' of someone's world and respecting it we are more likely to gain access into it which in turn enables us to support and facilitate change in others. DeLozier (1987) refers to an old Native American proverb - never judge anyone until you have walked a mile in their moccasins.

7 **Not all interactions in a system are on the same level. What is positive on one level may be negative on another level. It is useful to separate behaviour from 'self', to separate the positive intention, function, belief etc, that generates the behaviour from the behaviour itself**
or
People are not their behaviours.

As soon as we provide a description to someone it can become part of their subjective experience and may influence how they think about how they are as a person. Individuals are much more than their behaviour and we are presented with a choice of either providing feedback on someone's behaviour or labelling their identity. If we review the example of exams there is a considerable difference between considering the behaviour of 'When I go into an exam room, I feel anxious and concerned about how I might answer the questions' compared to 'I am a failure'. The first statement describes at a behavioural level the thoughts and feelings of the individual, the second statement labels their identity as a failure. In coaching work with clients it is often useful to consider behaviours that they want to change and adapt rather than focus on feedback that they have had at identity level. An example of this was a client who was told that she was 'loud and noisy' in the office. She assumed that this meant that her personality was loud and that this was unprofessional and hence became confused and upset by this. Whereas if she had been offered feedback that said 'at times you speak loudly while on the phone and it can be distracting for others, so can you take some of your calls in an office rather than the open plan area', she would have understood which of her behaviours required modification and would have avoided the feelings and thinking that she experienced.

8 **At some level all behaviour is (or was at one time) 'positively intended' and people make the best choices available to them, given the possibilities and capabilities that they perceive available to them from their model of the world**
or
Every behaviour has a positive intention.

This presupposition emerged from Erickson's work who literally relabelled what people did to encourage change, so instead of a problem being perceived as a difficulty, it was reframed as an asset. Many examples of this are given in Rosen's book (1992). As an observer to someone else's behaviour we may not view it as positive yet if we were to imagine becoming the other person through second position (described in chapter 5) we will be able to see that the behaviour will have a positive intent for the individual.

9 The processes that take place within a person, and between people and their environment, are systemic. Our bodies, our societies and our universe form an ecology of systems and subsystems all of which interact with and mutually influence each other
or
Behaviour and change are to be evaluated in terms of context and ecology.

This presupposition comes from Bateson's (1979) work on ecology and systems theory. He held the view that the mind operates with an ecological system and that the ecology of an individual is made up of the mind, body, relationships and interrelationships. Wherever ideas, change or interventions are offered into the system they act like seeds being introduced into the environment. They can only root, grow and flourish if the system is supportive. If the system is not supportive, the seeds may die away or may even act as toxins within the system, causing chaos to occur.

10 It is not possible to completely isolate any part of a system from the rest of the system. People cannot not influence each other and people respond to their own perceptions of reality
or
You can't not communicate.

Irrespective of how much we try not to communicate our thoughts and feelings we will give away information in our unconscious communication. This is considered further in chapter 4 when we look at sensory acuity. As we communicate unconsciously we can alter another person's view of their reality. In reviewing the 'exam' scenario discussed earlier we can see how this system can be easily influenced by different versions of reality amongst the models of the world that make it up. The youngster taking the exam may, in a falsetto voice, respond to his mother's enquiry on how the exam went, that the exam was 'fine'.

The mother interprets this and in hushed tones later on will tell father that the son was struggling. Father then tries to hide this concern and acts as if everything is fine. The son sees father being over friendly and from this out of the norm behaviour, assumes his father thinks he has failed, so goes into a deeper spiral of worry while waiting for his results. This is only one possible scenario and many more meanings and roles can be acted out here to demonstrate that, irrespective of how we might try to hide what we are experiencing, somewhere in our unconscious communication we literally 'give the game away'. In sales and negotiation meetings this is often referred to as the 'tell', that lets the negotiator know his opponents weak spot.

11 Systems are 'self organising' and naturally seek states of balance and stability. There are no failures, only feedback.

Again based in Bateson's work on ecology this presupposition assumes that as each system is self organising, feedback will arise that will enable the system to remain in a state of equilibrium. This happens at levels that are often below conscious awareness. Examples of this are when a coaching client struggles again and again to get promotion and keeps failing. They then take a change in direction for their career and suddenly doors open in ways that they had not anticipated.

This presupposition is sometimes viewed as it not being 'ok' to see things as failure and it being important to view the learning from a situation such that an alternative course of action can be taken. Occasionally a client may have a secondary gain for experiencing failures, i.e., they are gaining a benefit from not succeeding at something. This is discussed further in considering outcomes in chapter 3.

12 The law of requisite variety – the part of the system with the most flexibility of behaviour will be the controlling or catalytic element in the system
or
The person with the most flexibility will control the system.

Bateson continues to influence the presuppositions through his work on cybernetics and systems theory. This presupposition encourages the NLPer to develop as much flexibility in behaviour as possible to enable them to have the most amount of influence over the system and using this behavioural flexibility to facilitate change in the system that they are operating in. Additionally, the more that we can facilitate others to develop greater flexibility of behaviour the more control they will have over their own system.

13 **People already have (or potentially have) all of the resources they need to act effectively.**

This presupposition formed the basis of Erickson's work, with him working from the principle that not only do people have all the resources that they need, but also that people are not broken and therefore do not need fixing. By expanding an understanding of the territory of the client it is possible to enable the client to identify and access resources that perhaps they had forgotten about, had not used for some time, or had not considered in another context. Returning to the 'exam' scenario, the youngster may not experience fear while out mountain biking down a steep hill, which, if the state is mapped into his current state of fear prior to exams, can be used to collapse the anchor of fear in the context of examinations. (See chapter 6 on how this can be done).

14 **The 'wisest' and most 'compassionate' maps are those which make available the widest and richest number of choices, as opposed to being the most 'real' or 'accurate'**
or
All procedures should increase choice and develop great personal flexibility.

Bateson continues to influence the work of NLP and as a colleague of Erickson it is difficult to determine if Bateson's views were influenced by Erickson or vice versa as both of them operated from this presupposition. The aim in NLP work is to ensure that the client leaves in as equal or better state with more choices than when they arrived. NLP considers 'how' things are and how they might be different. By looking at this choice is opened up to clients in new and different ways. Asking our 'exam' scenario student 'why' he is fearful will no doubt elicit lots of reasons about failing before, not feeling good enough and so on, and may spiral into an unuseful feeling of lack of self worth by the end of a coaching session. Whereas if we ask the question 'how' does he 'do' fear for exams and how does he 'not do' fear of mountain biking, he will start to think about his behaviours and strategies (chapter 6) in different contexts which will give him access to more choice in behavioural response for him.

15 **Individual skills are a function of the development and sequencing of representational systems**
or
If one person can do it, anybody can.

By eliciting and understanding an individual's strategy for a behaviour it is possible to replicate it for ourselves. The presupposition refers to utilising the existing resources of an individual and it is probably sensible to assume that this presupposition takes into account unalterable factors such as gender, physical stature, age et. This presupposition is based in modelling and enables the components of performance excellence that is highlighted by Churches in education, Walker in health and Lazarus in sports earlier in this chapter. It is by understanding the precise sequencing and utilisation of representational systems that enables a person to get the results that they get, and in modelling this for ourselves and others we can replicate these results.

Cause and Effect

Perception is
Projection

Principles of cause and effect
& perception is projection

Bateson (1972/2000) influenced both of these philosophical principles of NLP through his reading of Jung's work. He found meaning in Jung's 'Seven Sermons to the Dead' and particularly the two worlds of thought, pleroma and creatora. Pleroma is the world of no distinction and is the world of effect, where we attribute meaning to things that we experience, i.e. there is no difference between us and our reality, we literally project what we perceive. Creatura is the world of difference and cause, where we can accurately identify with differences that are effective, i.e. we can determine the elements that are effective and are not influenced by our subjectivity.

Cause and Effect. Bateson identified this process as one of power and control that individuals will use in their behaviour to ensure that they stay in control. Causal thinking places you at choice in how you respond to situations. You can make excuses and blame others so that any possible solutions will become the responsibility of the other person. You then appear powerless and remain at the Effect of the situation. Alternatively you can take responsibility to respond to the situation in the most resourceful way and empower yourself to be part of the solution, thereby being at Cause.

One of the useful ways to consider Cause and Effect is to think about the language that individuals use.

Cause	Effect
Responsibility	Reasons
Empowered	Excuses
Ownership	Justification
'Yes'	'Yes but'
'I can'	'It's the ...'

Perception is Projection. Building on Jung's theory that stimulated some of Bateson's thinking, it is important to go back and review Freud's definition of the mechanism of perception, 'Verneinung', which he viewed as a judgement that we use to act as a barrier to stimuli that we can't accept because of repressed fears or desires. We literally create our reality based on our projection of our subjective experience onto the world around us. Whatever we fear inside ourselves we will see in others and project this attribute on to them, both positive and negative. This often results in individuals attracting towards them the things that they fear the most. Think about a summer's day in the garden, isn't it interesting how the wasps only bother the people who are fearful of them? We may also deny in ourselves our strongest most positive attributes because we fear them, for example we may see other people as strong, powerful, beautiful or successful and yet would not apply these same descriptors to ourselves.

One of the quotes that I find inspiring is that by Marianne Williamson that begins

Our deepest fear is not that
we are inadequate.
Our deepest fear is that we
are powerful beyond measure.

Chapter Three

Goal Setting and Outcomes

Getting to know NLP

ONE OF the aspects of NLP that sets it apart from other models of psychologically based interventions is that it is outcome focussed. NLP focuses on what is possible for the client and assumes success and the application of successful strategies to a future oriented way of being.

By focussing on the outcome it allows you to:

- Compare where you are now with where you want to be so you can create the most beneficial opportunities

- Take responsibility for the problem and empower yourself to move toward a solution

- Assess your progress and to establish when you have achieved the outcome

- Create purpose and make your outcome even more compelling

Rationale for outcome setting and the use of goals

There are a number of theories that underpin the effectiveness of goal setting. These are based in neuroscience, social development and psychological development.

The neuroscience theory

Goal setting presupposes that a solution exists for the problem state, or if no problem exists, that there is a more effective/successful way of achieving something, particularly in performance related goals. This process stimulates the reticular activation system (RAS) which is responsible for self regulation, activation of arousal towards motivational states and organised mental activity (Solms 1996).

Additionally, the goal setting process of NLP requires the client to visualise attainment of their goal, which accesses the full potential of the reticular activation system through an increase in arousal and attention responses, including what we pay attention to consciously. This stimulates the client's nervous system towards goal seeking behaviour. As the reticular activation system is accessed neuropeptides are released resulting in increased blood flow to the area of the body responsible for attainment of the goal. When we consider how effective visualisation processes are proven to be for sports performance, presentations and for health related matters, it is now clear that the increased oxygenation that is activated through this increased circulation to crucial areas is one key to enabling goal attainment.

Social learning theory

As soon as we think about goal activation and utilising the neuroscience components of arousal and attention responses, there are theories that add to this from social development: classical and operant conditioning and social learning theory. The processes of utilising conditioning theory are covered in chapter 6. Pavlov's (1904/1927) classic conditioning work with dogs demonstrated positive and negative responses to unusual stimuli, and that it was possible to eliminate these stimuli using a similar process. Watson and Reyner (1920) transferred the early work of Pavlov to understanding fear responses in infants and were able to replicate the elimination of fear in the infants. Skinner's (1938) operant conditioning theory helped to gain understanding of the pleasure and pain principle, that we develop generalised behavioural responses towards behaviour that results in pleasant consequences, and the opposite happens where this does not occur. In more recent years Pert (1997) added to the theory with her views on state dependent recall - a person is more likely to recall positive experiences when in a good state and negative experiences when in a bad state. Bandura (1977) developed social learning theory out of his understanding of classic and operant conditioning. He proposed that children will copy behaviour if they see this behaviour being rewarded, the model is similar to them, that there is some power or control over the desired object and that they are warm and nurturing. His theory included a greater understanding of the modelling process and that success was more likely if the individual focussed only on certain aspects of the model, was able to accurately hold the model in their memory, could accurately copy the model's behaviour, all of which resulted in motivation to maintain the behaviour to gain the reward.

Psychological and emotional development

Within early psychological and emotional development the reticular activation system is developed in direct response to care giver interaction. The first instances of goal oriented behaviour are seen in infants as young as 3 months (Stern 1998).

Evidence base

I have been able to find only one study that evidences overall outcomes in NLPt and one study that utilises the outcome frame to facilitate change in NLP therapy. There is also a study that utilises the outcome frame alongside other NLP interventions in an educational setting.

Weaver (2009) has conducted research that set out to measure his clients' overall experience of neurolinguistic psychotherapy using the CORE (clinical outcomes in routine evaluation) model. CORE is a standardised tool that audits, evaluates and measures the outcomes of clients in therapy by creating numerical scores that quantify the level of problems and distress experienced by the client. His findings demonstrated a statistical and clinically significant reduction in the pre and post CORE scores and in the severity rating scores of problems.

Gray (2009) has utilised the well formed outcome frame to assist clients access a preferred future state using Prochaska's (1992) model for change. His research with offenders with various levels of substance use disorders included the use of the well formed outcome frame to identify a preferred future that was meaningful. Using submodality and anchoring techniques, the results of the programme demonstrated that 30% of participants where abstinent one year following treatment. Additionally participants reported increased positive affect, self efficacy and general satisfaction as a result of the programme. Statistical results show that the NLP interventions were equivalent to those achieved in intensive outpatient care, and were less expensive in time and cost.

Squirrel (2009) utilised future pacing in her work with young children displaying social, emotional and behavioural difficulties. Findings of her experimental study suggest that some NLP techniques are useful with this group and in comparing the trial group to the control group, there was an improvement in behaviour.

The recent research into mirror neurons (Gallese 1996), and the understanding of learning through imitation, links directly into the modelling component of NLP. Mirror neurons are activated when we take action (one of the 5 pillars of success, and some of the achievement component of the PACER model), and also when observing someone else taking an action that we want to do (resources of the PACER model). If you know someone who can already 'do' the outcome then it is much easier to model their behaviour and increase the potential of you being successful yourself by 'mimicking' them. This activates the mirror neurons that will then drive the behaviour required rather than you learning how to do something from the beginning.

Psychologist Locke (1968) was one of the first to research the goal setting and motivational factors in a general management context. His early research demonstrated that conscious goal setting was an effective motivator. Specifically, he identified that hard goals are more likely to produce results particularly regarding output. Interestingly, monetary incentives, time limits and knowledge of results do not affect performance level where this is independent of the individual's goals and intentions.

Tubbs (1986) has conducted a meta-analysis of evidence to support Locke's goal theory. A meta-analysis is a review of multiple research studies to gain an overview of existing evidence for something. The results of these studies demonstrate that the theory was supported although the setting of the studies and the process by which the goal setting factors were utilised were considered to be variables.

To summarise Locke's findings over many years of researching goals, success and motivation (Locke and Latham 1990)

    „ Goals that challenge lead to higher performance than easy goals. Goals set at moderately difficult levels are most motivating.

    „ Specific goals are more effective than 'do your best' goals. Individuals can measure their performance.

    „ Feedback allows individuals to adjust their behaviour so that they remain on target for goal achievement

    „ Proximal goals are more motivating than distal goals. Proximal provide a marker of progress in the short-term, distal goals are too remote to give incentive.

Ordóñez et al (2009) challenge some of Locke's recommendations and findings on goal setting and propose that goal setting has powerful effects and at the same time can have negative side effects. Specifically, in an unpublished draft paper, they propose that 'there is mounting causal evidence linking goal setting with a range of behaviors including a shift in risk taking (Larrick, Heath and Wu, in press), greater unethical behaviour (Schweitzer, Ordóñez, and Douma 2004), and a narrow focus that draws attention from other important elements of the problem (Staw and Boettger 1990). Ordóñez et al. (2009) cite these and other empirically-based articles that demonstrate a causal link between goal setting and harmful behavior' (p. 5). This paper was later published in revised form.

Principles of goal setting

Goal setting utilises the principles of the 5 pillars of success and assumes that if we apply each of these components to our goal setting, we are more likely to achieve success.

- **Outcome orientation** enables you to focus on where you want to go and make it less likely that you will find yourself distracted by other factors
- Have **sensory acuity** so that you are aware of the impact of your actions and ensure that you know when you are getting the results that you want. Be specific about what you see, hear and feel as a result of the action you have taken. The more aware you are, the more you can take appropriate action to ensure you achieve your outcome.
- Be flexible with your behaviour. **Behavioural flexibility** means giving yourself more choices and using as many ways as you need to, to achieve your outcome
- **Take action**. No matter how well formed your outcome is you need to take action to get results.
- **Operate from a physiology and psychology of excellence**. Manage your thoughts and feelings (state) so that you stay at your most resourceful to achieve your outcome .

Process of goal setting

Goal setting works by considering some of the well formed conditions that are considered to be necessary to enable the outcome to be achieved. These are very simple and include consideration of:

- Stated positively. The unconscious mind is unable to process negative linguistic terms, therefore if the client says 'I don't want to be poor' or 'I don't want to fail', the message that the unconscious hears will delete the 'not' and will hear 'I want to be poor' or 'I want to fail'. Freud refers to this process as verneinung - a process whereby a client will deny things 'you ask who this person in the dream can be. It's not his mother'. We emend this to; 'so it is his mother'. (Freud 1904 p. 235). If goals are stated in the positive – 'I want to be wealthy', or 'I want to succeed', the unconscious mind creates a representation of 'being wealthy' or 'succeeding' and activates the neural pathways that are directly related to the achievement of this behaviour.

∞ Sensory specific. By stating the goal using sensory specific terms this triggers the reticular activation system and stimulates the arousal and attention responses, thereby facilitating a behavioural response that is directly linked to attainment of the goal.

∞ Start and maintain. Can the client start and maintain the process of the steps required to achieve the goal? If they are unable to do this the goal may need to be changed to something that they can start and maintain, or they may decide to develop some skills or conduct some preparatory work before they set the goal.

∞ Contextualised. Is the client able to place the goal in context, both within the here and now and also within the context of other goals in their life? Considering the context for the goal also ensures that some of the ecological conditions are met such as where and when they want the goal, or in which contexts would the goal not be useful.

∞ Positive by-products. In all behaviour there is a positive intention for the individual otherwise they would not do the behaviour. There may be some positive aspects of the existing behaviour that the person wants to keep. It is important to think about these positive by-products and ensure that they are included in the goal setting, thereby making it easier to change and achieve the goal.

∞ Ecology. Does the goal support the individual in terms of cost and the time required to achieve it? Does the goal support the overall sense of self, wider relationships and other areas of the individual's life? Sometimes we can decide that we want something such as new job or career move and we may not consider this goal according to what else might be going on in our life.

Procedure

The procedure for goal setting is a straightforward coaching process. One of the mnemonics used for this is PACER; other models are found across the field of NLP.

Step	Question	Comments
1. Positive	*What do you want?* *What will this bring you?*	It is important that the client states what they want and not what they don't want. If the client presents a negative, then ask the question, 'what do you want instead?' Sometimes clients will want a goal that is low level and may only be environmental, e.g. 'I want a new computer'. By asking the question, 'what will this bring you?' the client is required to chunk up and expand their focus to the benefits, e.g. greater flexibility to balance my working life
2. Achievement	*How will you know when you are succeeding?* *How will you know when you have got it?* *What will you see, hear and feel?* *How will someone else know when you have got it?* *What is the first step?* *What is the last step?*	This will activate the neural pathway directly responsible for motivational behaviours required for achievement of the goal. By visualising evidence of achievement of the goal, it is as if it has already happened, and the client will develop an internal image of achievement of the goal. This activates the RAS and particularly the visual component. This encourages the client to dissociate from achievement of the goal thereby enhancing the motivation towards the achievement of it. By remaining dissociated from something that we want, the more desirable it becomes. Think about a favourite food; imagine it in front of you, still in its wrapper, or on the plate. Now imagine the empty wrapper or plate. Which is more desirable? Begins to activate the neural pathways and behaviours that are directly responsible for achievement of the goal. Links the neurological pathway through to direct attainment of the goal, from first to last step

3. Context	*When, where and with whom do you want it?* *When, where and with whom do you not want it?* *How long for?*	There may be some situations where the goal is inappropriate and may result in activation of a fear or anxiety response, leading to 'away from' behaviours e.g. I worked with a client who wanted promotion to Director level in his organisation. On working with him on his goal, this question elicited very clear criteria of where he would want to take up the position. As he thought about it he realised that the post would mean that he would need to work away from his home town several nights each week. His wife was a hospital Consultant and she relied on him being home by 6pm to look after their children when she was required to be on call. He decided to refocus his goal to something that was more ecological for the family
4. Ecology	*What time will this outcome need?* *Who else is affected and how will they feel?* *How does it fit in with your other outcomes?* *How does it increase your choices?* *What will happen if you get it?* *What won't happen if you get it?* *What will happen if you don't get it?* *What won't happen if you don't get it?*	The client will want to consider how achieving the outcome will affect the wider system. It may have an impact on resources such as finance and time. It may have an impact on other people, on other roles they play in their life and on the choices it gives them as outlined in the client above. These four questions are specifically designed to identify if the client has a secondary gain, or too many positive by-products to make the change. They are based in quantum linguistics (Chen 2002) and will facilitate the freeing up of linguistic double binds if they are asked of the client. (Wake 2008, p. 98-101)

5. Resources	*Can you start and maintain it?*	This condition is about how much direct control the person has over the achievement of the outcome and how much other people will be involved. There is little point in the client working on goals that they have little direct control over. This enables utilisation of social learning theory, by encouraging modelling of a successful other
	What resources have you already got? (Skills, people, money, objects etc.)	
	What resources do you need?	
	Who has already succeeded in achieving this outcome?	

Exercise

Spend some time thinking about an outcome that you want to achieve. Use the PACER model as it is outlined to set your goal. You may want to work with a coach to ask you the questions.

Step	Question	Response
1. Positive	*What do you want?*	
	What will this bring you?	

2. Achievement	How will you know when you are succeeding?	
	How will you know when you have got it?	
	What will you see, hear and feel?	
	How will someone else know when you have got it?	
	What is the first step?	
	What is the last step?	
3. Context	When, where and with who do you want it?	
	When, where and with who do you not want it?	
	How long for?	

4. Ecology	*What time will this outcome need?*
	Who else is affected and how will they feel?
	How does it fit in with your other outcomes?
	How does it increase your choices?
	What will happen if you get it?
	What won't happen if you get it?
	What will happen if you don't get it?
	What won't happen if you don't get it?
5. Resources	*Can you start and maintain it?*
	What resources have you already got? (Skills, people, money, objects etc.)
	What resources do you need?
	Who has already succeeded in achieving this outcome?

Applications

Goal setting has many applications and can be used as an individual coaching tool; a group goal setting exercise; a process for determining realistic outcomes in individuals with chronic health conditions; for couples, families and individuals in therapy work; for businesses and business leaders; for sports enthusiasts and professionals; for teachers, children and educators.

Chapter Four

Understanding other people

Begining to unserstand others

EFFECTIVE COMMUNICATORS have a fluidity and flexibility within their approach that means they are able to communicate effectively with anyone. They are excellent at being able to read and interpret the communication responses that they receive from their audience and can adapt their own communication style in direct response to different individuals.

In this section I cover the four elements that enable effective communicators to respond to the world of others:

 Sensory Acuity, Rapport, Representational Systems and Eye Patterns.

Sensory acuity

As we have already discovered in the previous chapter, sensory acuity is one of the Pillars of Success and can be used to let you know when you are achieving something and when you need to change what you are doing. Having sensory awareness also enables you to notice more about how other people respond. By observing how people respond you can create and maintain rapport with them. We can also use sensory acuity to notice when a client has achieved their outcome.

Rationale

Sensory acuity was modelled from Erickson's ability to quickly calibrate moment to moment changes in the people that he worked with. This skill was developed as he was recovering from polio in his teens and he refers to his ability to notice the 'frequent… startling contradictions between the verbal and the non-verbal communications within a single interchange. This aroused so much my interest that I intensified my observations at every opportunity' (Bandler and Grinder 1975b p.vii).

When Erickson described these contradictions he was describing the sensory based information that he was observing. As our thinking changes our state will also change which will directly influence our behaviour (demonstrated within the Communication Model in chapter 2).

Evidence base

There are some studies that can demonstrate effectiveness of olfactory and tactile acuity however these do not measure the sensory acuity components of NLP, and are specific to subjects such as acuity in smell for industries such as the wine trade, and for touch in healing therapies. There are no research studies that support sensory acuity within NLP.

Principles of sensory acuity

Our state is dependent on our nervous system responses and whether we are responding with parasympathetic (relaxed) or sympathetic (flight/fright/fight) arousal. When the parasympathetic nervous system is stimulated an individual is usually in a relaxed state, blood is flowing to the periphery and there is a resultant physiological response that can be observed in factors such as skin colour, breathing rate, pupil dilatation. When the sympathetic nervous system is stimulated the individual responds from the flight/fright/fight responses, blood returns to the main organs of the body and the resultant physical response can be seen in a lightening of skin colour (people refer to someone going 'as white as a sheet'), an increase in breathing rate and the pupils become focussed. In observing an individual it is important to have sensory based evidence and use sensory descriptions to describe these observations rather than assume meaning from your observations, which would then be a mind read. In the previous sentence I have referred to 'lightening of skin colour' which is a sensory based description, whereas 'he is as white as a sheet' is a mind read. Other examples are:

Sensory	Mind Read
His breathing increased	He got excited
Her colour darkened	She blushed
His pupils dilated	He loved what he saw
Her voice got louder	She shouted

Process of sensory acuity

Sensory acuity is measured using a process referred to as Calibration. Calibration means to measure, to be able to calibrate the moment to moment changes that are apparent in someone's physiology as their state changes between the sympathetic and parasympathetic parts of their nervous system.

Procedure

The procedure for calibrating the changes in state in a client is to notice the changes that happen in another person as you ask them to think about different scenarios, e.g. someone they like and someone they don't like, or a food they like and a food they don't like. The main factors that we notice in calibration are listed below and each pairing will be on a spectrum, e.g. someone's skin colour can go from very dark to very light or could be somewhere in between.

Physiology	Sympathetic response	Parasympathetic response
Lower lip size	Lines	No lines
Eyes	Focussed	Defocussed
Pupil dilation	Constricted	Dilated
Breathing rate	Fast	Slow
Breathing location	High	Low
Skin tonus	Shiny	Not shiny
Skin colour	Light	Dark

Exercise

Find a colleague to work with.

Ask them to think of a person they like and observe each of the elements above. Notice where they are on the spectrum.

Ensure that they change their state by asking them to think of something neutral such as what they had for breakfast that day.

Now ask them to think of a person they don't like again observing each of the elements above. Notice any changes on the spectrum based on your previous observation.

Cont'd

Again, change their state by asking them to think of something neutral such as what they are having for dinner.

Ask them to select one of the two scenarios without telling you which one they have selected, either the person they like or the person they don't like.

Now calibrate and see if you can identify which person they are thinking of.

Once you think you are able to calibrate which person they are thinking of check with them to determine if you were accurate.

Applications

You can calibrate the moment to moment changes in many situations. I have suggested some for you to consider and that I know have been successful in various contexts.

Sales meetings – to determine whether they have a positive response to your product. One sales team in a fast moving consumer goods (FMCG) organisation were able to work out when their customer was becoming keen on the ideas that were presented to them in a sales negotiation meeting. They then used this information to ensure that they built on the positive response and were able to change their sales process quickly enough during the meeting to ensure that they got a close on the sale.

Appraisals – in determining how they are responding to your feedback.

Parenting – to observe how your children feel about different topics at school. One parent has used this to work out when her youngster was about to think about having a temper tantrum and was able to introduce a diversionary tactic to ensure that the anticipated behaviour did not occur. They were able to interrupt the pattern and this has become part of their strategy for dealing with problems that had been occurring.

Coaching – to calibrate how enthusiastic a coachee feels about a goal that they are discussing and to use this information to gain a greater understanding of the goal, making it more specific to the individual.

Education – to gather information about individual responses to your teaching style.

Sports – to assess levels of approval for a new exercise or training regime.

Rapport

Rapport is a process that many of us do naturally and is rarely taught formally in any of the social sciences such as coaching, therapy or HR. It is frequently taught in sales based training programmes. There are a number of definitions of rapport from the simple and self explanatory, 'People who are like each other, like each other', to the more comprehensive 'a process of responsiveness whereby the client's unconscious mind uncritically accepts suggestions offered to it'. Essentially rapport is about a relationship of trust with another person.

Rationale

Rapport was modelled from Erickson's matching of his clients' physiology, language and voice qualities. Even though Erickson was limited in his physical abilities he would utilise different aspects of his behaviour to match someone else's physiology, e.g. if a client was agitated and pacing up and down the room, Erickson would match the pacing and levels of agitation such as speed of speech with finger tapping or head nodding. His students also observed that he would be in trance himself as he put his clients into trance thereby leading them into deeper states of relaxation by using his own physiological processes. Rapport was also utilised by therapists such as Carl Rogers, Fritz Perls and Virginia Satir. In the video of *Gloria – 3 Approaches to Psychotherapy* there is evidence of how Rogers and Perls both used the process of rapport in therapy with the client.

Evidence base

A number of studies have been conducted that indicate similar findings in assessing which aspects of our communication have the most impact. Social Psychologist Argyle et al (1970) proposed that 55% of the meaning of a message is inferred by observing the physiology of another person, 38% meaning is inferred from the voice qualities that we hear, and only 7% by the words that are used. His studies identified that non-verbal communication has three main functions: conveying interpersonal information through body language; to support verbal communication with additional non-verbal signals such as grunts or head nods which offer and seek feedback; and to replace speech which is made difficult because of environmental factors such as noise or in a large group. Verbal communication is used for conveying factual information.

Mehrabian's (1967a, 1967b, 1971) research also supported the above findings, that total liking in face to face communication is 7%, verbally liking is

38% and facial liking is 55%. Critics of his study consider that his research was limited in that it was simplistic in design and only looked at student responses to 9 words, then 9 words with voice tonalities applied, then 9 words with voice tonalities and facial expressions applied.

Birdwhistell (1970) conducted research at a similar time and using films of interactions between individuals in a number of settings was able to demonstrate the interdependent relationship between movement, speech and non verbal communication.

Specifically to NLP, Sandhu et al (1991) have conducted a control trial assessing the impact of mirroring or non mirroring on empathy, trustworthiness and positive interaction in a cross-cultural setting. A validated assessment tool was used and findings suggest that mirroring of body movements results in an increase in perceptions of empathy.

Principles of rapport

Rapport works by developing attunement or responsiveness between the right hemisphere of the Communicator and the Subject. Communication literally occurs between the right hemisphere of one person to the right hemisphere of the other person, i.e. the unconscious of each individual communicates to the other. This has been demonstrated to successfully activate mirror neurons (Gallese et al 1996; Gallese & Goldman 1998; Rizzolatti et al, 1999; Gallese, 2001) the brain process that we use to unconsciously mimic behaviour in others and adopt this behaviour for ourselves.

How to develop rapport

There are a number of ways of developing rapport with another person. One simple way of doing this is to match their physiology, voice qualities and key words. By matching them you are doing the same as them, so if they raise their left arm you raise your left arm. Alternatively you can mirror their behaviour and it appears as if they are looking in a mirror, if they raise their left arm you raise your right arm. Another option is to match one part of your physiology to another part of their physiology e.g. if they are clicking their pen on and off you could tap your foot in time to the clicking. By matching or mirroring someone else's behaviour you will directly activate the mirror neurons and also the attunement or relationship centres of the brain and will set up unconscious communication. Once unconscious communication is established there are a number of indicators that you can notice. These include a feeling which some people describe as a warmth or that something has 'clicked'; a change in the skin colour of your client usually to a darker colour; the client says something e.g. 'Have we met before' or 'I feel as if I have known you for ever or could talk to you for ages'; and finally an ability to lead the other person, e.g. if you scratch your leg they will automatically copy you without being aware of it. This ability to lead someone else requires the individual to have initially built a conscious level of trust (rapport), sufficient to convince the unconscious mind to co-operate. Indeed, this 'leading' will only occur if they feel confident that the relationship of trust and rapport can only lead to outcomes that are helpful - that it's fundamentally 'OK' to be led. This 'self-defence' mechanism within the unconscious mind therefore avoids the potential risk of manipulating someone to do something that they don't want to do.

Procedure

In matching someone's physiology there are certain aspects that you can pay attention to:

- Breathing – rate and location
- Posture – whether standing or sitting
- Gestures – it would be less obvious if you were to match their gestures after they have used them and in a manner that suits your usual communication style
- Eye contact
- Facial expression
- Style of dress.

Matching voice qualities is effective and some of the elements that you would pay attention to are:

- Tone – particularly whether there is a high or low pitch
- Tempo – speed or rhythm of speech
- Timbre – the quality or resonance
- Volume.

In matching words, it is considered to be important to match:

- „ Key words and phrases – particularly words that have an emphasis
- „ Predicates – often the describing words that someone uses
- „ Common experiences
- „ Chunk size – speaking in detail or the abstract.

Exercise

Find a colleague to work with and assign the roles of Coach and Client.

Have a discussion about something that you are both comfortable with. During this time the coach will match the client's physiology and begin to disagree with the verbal content of the discussion. Notice the impact of the coach's behaviour on the client.

Continue the conversation and this time the coach will match the content of the conversation but mismatch the physiology of the client. Notice the impact of the coach's behaviour on the client.

Continue the conversation and this time match both the conversation and the physiology of the client. Notice the impact of the coach's behaviour on the client.

Applications

Sales – to unconsciously set up a feeling of trust with your customers. Going back to the sales team discussed in sensory acuity, the team decided to utilise rapport prior to the start of the meeting. One member of the sales team was designated to take responsibility for gaining rapport. A second member of the sales team was responsible for answering questions and providing data, and the third member backed up the rapport of the rapport leader. As the meeting progressed the team noticed that the customer team were beginning to also be in rapport with the sales team. The team increased their level of rapport and moved to leading, quickly agreeing a good price and were able to close with both parties being satisfied. It is important to note that individuals will only stay in rapport with you while their values or criteria for a purchase are being met. If a sales person tries to sell something that does not meet the criteria of an individual, the individual will either end the sales meeting without buying, or may get buyer's remorse and end up ending their relationship with you because they feel as if you have manipulated them.

Management – to set up unconscious responsiveness to your suggestions. A senior manager found that he was due to follow a speaker who had not gone down well with the audience at an organisational briefing. Rather than stand in the same place as the first speaker he stepped forward and suggested to the audience that as they had been sitting for a while, perhaps, they might like to stand up and stretch before he began his presentation. By getting them to stand up he was leading them into rapport with himself. This is a well known tool in the toolkit of motivational speakers.

HR – to open up dialogue and enable others to trust you in interviews or difficult personnel meetings.

Parenting – to enable your child to trust you with things that may be bothering them.

Coaching – to set up trust and responsiveness with your clients to enable them to achieve their outcomes.

Education – to lead learning and facilitate improved behaviour in the classroom by getting greater levels of responsiveness from students .

Sports – enabling your coachees to trust you and respond to your coaching.

Representational Systems

Representational systems

Representational systems are how we re-present our experience of the external world to ourselves. Within the communication model detailed in chapter 2, our representational system is how we code information within our nervous system as an Internal Representation. Within representational systems two terms of reference are used. Primary representational system is the system that a person uses over the others to process their experience of the world (Dilts and DeLozier 2000). Lead representational system is the system that a person uses to search for their representation of an experience, e.g. I may need to recall a visual image of my car (visual lead) to be able to access my experience of the sound of the engine.

Rationale

By understanding the preferred representational system of a client we are able to influence how we communicate to them so that they receive information in their preferred system. Bandler and Grinder observed that Satir would use representational systems to match or influence her client's experience during therapy and suggested that these systems are behavioural traits that we use to make sense of our world.

Evidence base

Bandler and Grinder (1976, 1979) proposed that representational systems are context dependent and that individuals will move between systems of neurological processing according to their relationship to the external environment.

Einspruch and Forman's (1985) study supports the contextualised nature of representational systems, proposing that previous studies to support the notion of specific preferred representational systems had inadequate controls that took into account this contextualisation. Bostic St. Clair and Grinder (2001) continue to reinforce the view that representational systems are context specific and can only be viewed from the perspective of how the individual is currently processing information.

Internal Primary Lead

Principles of representational systems

We experience the world through our senses, we see, hear, feel, taste, or smell things happening outside ourselves. We also represent those experiences internally in the same way i.e. we will remember them as images, sounds, feeling, tastes and smells. In representing our world through our senses we use different aspects of each of our senses. There is a school of thought that suggests population percentages for each of the systems: 40% are thought to prefer images, 40% are thought to prefer feelings, taste and smell and 20% are thought to prefer sounds or self talk. There is no evidence for these figures and within certain populations and in my experience of working with many groups there appear to be generalisations e.g. telesales people tend to prefer auditory, scientists tend to prefer auditory digital, artists tend to prefer visual or kinaesthetic.

❧ Visual	**External** – what we see outside
	Internal – what we visualise inside
❧ Auditory	**External** – what we hear outside
	Internal – sounds that we remember
	Auditory Digital – how you talk to yourself
❧ Kinaesthetic	**External** – tactile – touch, temperature, moisture
	Internal – visceral – emotions and internal feelings
	Internal – proprioceptive – muscle memory of position or motion
❧ Olfactory	**Smells**
❧ Gustatory	**Tastes**

Process of identifying the primary representational system

There are a number of indicators that will help you identify someone's primary representational system. You may find that some people fit into more than one category or use more than one system at a time. It can be useful to think about the one that they use for the majority of the time.

Visual representational system is the process of translating communication into pictures. An individual will tend to stand or sit with their heads and/or bodies erect and with their eyes looking up. They usually breathe quite fast and from the top of their lungs and they use fast gestures often around the upper region of their body or in the air. Their appearance is important to them and they tend to be organised and neat. They memorise by seeing pictures and are less distracted by noise, and they may have trouble remembering verbal instructions because their minds tend to wander. Their speed of speech is quite fast to match their breathing rate. Their language will use pictorial descriptions and they must see something to understand it.

Auditory representational system is the process of translating communication into sounds. Someone who is processing information using their auditory system will tend to move their eyes sideways and breathe from the middle of their chest. They can often be observed talking to themselves. They are easily distracted by noise and will be able to repeat things back to you easily. They learn by listening, enjoy music, talking on the phone and will respond to a certain tone of voice or set of words. They memorise by steps, procedures, and sequences. They tend to speak at a medium to fast rate.

Kinaesthetic representational system is the process of checking communication with feelings. Someone who is processing information using their kinaesthetic system will breathe from the bottom of their lungs and you will often see their abdomen move as they breathe. They will tend to move and talk quite slowly and are responsive to physical rewards and touch. They memorise things by walking them through or doing them and will usually check out their feelings prior to expressing thoughts. This system also includes the use of olfactory and gustatory senses.

Auditory digital representational system is the process of checking communication with ourselves. Individuals will spend time talking to their selves and making sense of things. They tend to speak in monotone and breathing patterns tend to be high up in the chest, more like an auditory processor. They are dissociated or detached from their feelings and will often be good in a crisis. They will exhibit characteristics of the other major representational systems.

Procedure

There are a number of ways to identify somebody's representational system including paying attention to the words that they use, their body language and breathing rate. Some of the words and phrases that people use to indicate how they are currently experiencing their world are summarised here:

Visual:	See, look, imagine, watch, dark, reveal, illuminate, glimpse, perceive
	Sight for sore eyes; pretty as a picture; make a show of; blind spot
Auditory:	Listen, hear, converse, resonate, silence, humming, harmony, quiet
	Sounds right to me; loud and clear; rings a bell; make music together
Kinaesthetic:	Touch, feel, soft, smooth, rough, hard, brittle, concrete, rub, harsh
	Touch base; get to grips with; stiff upper lip; warm hearted, soft touch
Auditory digital:	Consider, evaluate, decide, interpret, analyse, process, sense, know
	Make sense of; to my mind; factual assessment; consider the options

It is also possible to identify the system that someone is preferring to use through a simple questionnaire. It is important to note that the scores in the questionnaire will reflect their current preferred mode of processing and that this can change in different contexts.

Test yourself

The representational system preference test

For each of the following statements, **please place a number next to every phrase.** Use the following system to indicate your preferences:

4 = Closest to describing you   **2** = Next best

3 = Next best description   **1** = Least descriptive of you

1

I make important decisions based on:

gut level feelings.

which way sounds the best.

what looks best to me.

precise review and study of the issues.

2

During an argument, I am most likely to be influenced by:

the other person's tone of voice.

whether or not I can see the other person's argument.

the logic of the other person's argument.

whether or not I feel I am in touch with other person's true feelings.

3

I most easily communicate what is going on with me by:

the way I dress and look.

the feelings I share.

the words I choose.

the tone of my voice.

4 **It is easiest for me to:**

☐ find the ideal volume and tuning on a stereo system.

☐ select the most intellectually relevant point concerning an interesting subject.

☐ select the most comfortable furniture.

☐ select rich, attractive colour combinations.

5

☐ I am very attuned to the sounds of my surroundings.

☐ I am very adept at making sense of new facts and data.

☐ I am very sensitive to the way articles of clothing feel on my body.

☐ I have a strong response to colours and to the way a room looks.

Scoring the representational preferences

STEP ONE:

Copy your answers from the test to the lines below.

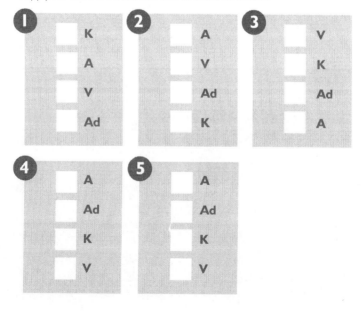

1
☐ K
☐ A
☐ V
☐ Ad

2
☐ A
☐ V
☐ Ad
☐ K

3
☐ V
☐ K
☐ Ad
☐ A

4
☐ A
☐ Ad
☐ K
☐ V

5
☐ A
☐ Ad
☐ K
☐ V

STEP TWO: Add the numbers associated with each letter.
There will be five entries for each letter.

	V	A	Ad	K
1				
2				
3				
4				
5				
TOTALS				

STEP THREE:
The comparison of the totalled scores gives the relative preference for each of the four major representational systems at the time that the individual was conducting the test.

Exercise

Spend some time listening to individuals in a meeting. Notice the words that they use and if there is a preference for one system above the others as they consider specific contexts. Once you identify their preferred system, ask a question using words from the same system to notice the impact.

Applications

Sales – to market and sell the product using each of the representational systems e.g. car sales – bright and clean body work, enable the customer to listen to the engine and sit inside the car, facts and figures booklet to detail specification etc.

Management – to communicate bulletins in the different formats, notice board or clear email communication to visual, focus groups or telephone calls to auditory, one to one chats with kinaesthetic, detailed email to auditory digital.

Parenting – develop each of the systems through games: colouring in and eye-spy for visual, rhyming games and songs for auditory, object guessing games for kinaesthetic; puzzles for auditory digital.

Sports – visualisation exercises to develop goal setting capacity and activation of the reticular activation system, use of music to motivate, spatial awareness exercises and fine motor movement to develop kinaesthetic acuity.

Eye Assessing Cues

Eye accessing cues

Eye patterns were first identified by Bandler and Grinder in 1976 and reported by Dilts and DeLozier (2000). Certain generalisations in eye movements were noticed and it was thought that these could provide an indication of how people are thinking.

Rationale

Eye accessing cues act as clues to the thinking process of others. It is thought that when people look up they are making pictures, when they look to either side in the midline they are thinking about sounds, and when they look down they are processing feelings or thoughts about feelings. There is also some thought about the use of remembered/past or constructed/future memories within the accessing cues.

Evidence base

Diamantopoulus et al (2009) have conducted a critical review of past research into eye accessing cues. Of the ten studies that research eye accessing cues, six studies have unsupportive results and that in reviewing the studies in depth, Diamantopoulus et al concluded that the validity and reliability of the results was poor. They summarise their extensive review with the proposal that 'there is no research that directly proves or disproves the EAC model and there is substantial ground for further research' (2009 p.7). They also make some interesting assumptions regarding the model (p.18).

- Questions should be subject specific and require refinement of the understanding of representational systems

- Rating of eye movements should be conducted by a machine

- All eye movements are relevant, there are a variable number of movements and they will be idiosyncratic with secondary generic patterns

- Staring equates with visual access or no trans-derivational search

- The baseline is indicative of auditory access or no trans-derivational search

- Distinctions can be made between eye movements that are visual and those that are non-visual

- Rapport is a necessary condition for eye accessing cues to be elicited

- Cultural and native background is significant

- Eye movements and physiological responses are significant.

Principles of eye accessing cues

We use our eyes as a way of internalising our external experience of the world via the thalamus. The thalamus is responsible for receiving all sensory information and will hold visual and auditory information as associated memory circuits. When an individual receives information they will process this information in the form of thoughts and images, including representations of primary experience. The visual processing system provides a connection between the sensory motor, emotional and cognitive areas of the brain and it is through visualisation that we make sense of meaning. Short et al (2005) have identified that we use multiple sensory stimuli of visual, auditory and kinaesthetic systems to create multiple implicit memories.

Process of eye accessing

You can calibrate someone's eye accessing cues by asking a series of questions and watching their eye movements as they answer. They will usually respond within a generalised pattern and it is important to note that each person's eye accessing cues are generalisations for them and they may not fit the wider generalisation. Some of the facets to consider in using eye accessing is to notice the lead representational system. This is the representational system that the person uses to lead the information that they require from their unconscious to their conscious processing.

Occasionally individuals will go through a process referred to as a transderivational search – literally to seek meaning across a number of different experiences which results in them accessing information from a number of different representational systems.

In some instances it may be difficult to observe eye accessing cues particularly if the client has a look to talk rule. This occurs in individuals who have learnt they must look at a person when they talk to them resulting in minimal eye movements.

Other individuals may use more than one system at the same time particularly when multiple senses make up the meaning of the experience. This is referred to as a synaesthesia.

There is some unproven suggestion that some individuals will also appear to be reverse organised. There is no empirical evidence to support this and Bandler and Grinder (1979) and Diamantopoulos (2009) propose that patterns are independent of handedness.

look to talk rule
transderivational search
synaesthesia

Procedure

The procedure for understanding eye patterns can either be to observe someone's eye movements as they are talking or utilise the eye pattern chart and questions, observing their responses.

Find someone to work with and ask them the following questions while observing their eye movements.

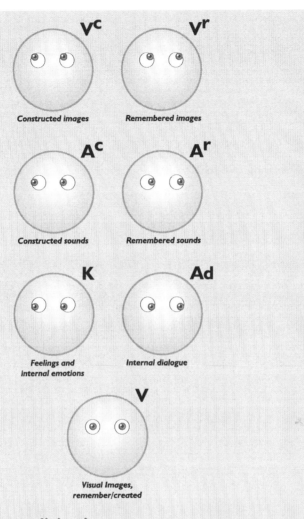

Vᶜ — Constructed images

Vʳ — Remembered images

Aᶜ — Constructed sounds

Aʳ — Remembered sounds

K — Feelings and internal emotions

Ad — Internal dialogue

V — Visual Images, remember/created

Eye pattern elicitation

Vᴿ	What colour was your first bicycle?
Vᶜ	What would your house look like if it was painted lime green?
Aᴿ	Can you recall the sound of your mother's voice?
Aᶜ	What would I sound like if I had Mickey Mouse's voice?
K	What does it feel like to put on wet socks?
Ad	Can you recite your 13 times table in your head?

Applications

Management – to observe eye patterns and utilise the cues to aid prompts and questions. E.g. if a colleague is struggling to answer a question and is looking up, you could ask the question 'what might it look like?

HR – to calibrate when someone is getting lost in feeling and is unable to communicate effectively. You may decide that it is appropriate to introduce a break in the session to give them time to gather their thoughts.

Parenting – to teach simple processes such as spelling using visual recall. By holding up the word in their visual recall area of accessing and ensuring they are in a positive state, they will be able to recall the information clearly next time they need it.

Coaching – to use a process of overlapping to aid solution based thinking. Overlapping uses a process of moving someone from the kinaesthetic system through the auditory and up to the visual. The coach commences by matching the language and physiology of the kinaesthetic processing of the coachee and then gradually introduces auditory language and physiology. When the coachee follows the lead of the coach, the coach can then introduce visual language and physiology.

Education – to ensure that all notice boards and education material is taught into the visual field. Where children access a negative feeling and then are required to look down to store their learning, this will become neurologically linked to the feeling.

Never judge another man until you have walked a mile in his moccasins

Native American Proverb

Chapter Five

Viewing Things from Alternative Perspectives

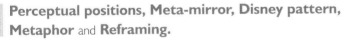

INDIVIDUALS WHO are able to successfully manage their interactions with other people and develop a win:win solution are excellent at viewing situations from a number of different perspectives. They are able to step into the world of another person with ease to understand what is going on. They frequently have high levels of intuition and can see alternative viewpoints to situations and will also use creative thinking to solve problems. Additionally they utilise their rapport skills to communicate directly with the unconscious mind of their audience working with metaphor to capture the attention of their audience. In this chapter I will review a number of processes that enable the development of intuitive understanding and insight into different situations through the use of :

Perceptual positions, Meta-mirror, Disney pattern, Metaphor and **Reframing.**

Perceptual positions

When a situation troubles us or we become stuck in our thinking we are often viewing things from only one perspective – our own. We become emotionally held in a particular position and find it difficult to dissociate ourselves sufficiently to see things from someone else's point of view. Individuals who are able to negotiate, manage conflict and find resolution where there are differing points of view are able to step out of their own world. They can step into someone else's world and are also able to distance themselves from the emotion and form an impartial view of what is occurring.

Rationale

John Grinder and Judith DeLozier (1987) developed perceptual positions as an extension of the early linguistic modelling by Bandler and Grinder of the meta-model (see chapter 8). This process enabled a spatial sort for changing the referential index of an experience, so, that, instead of viewing things from your own reference (first person referential index) you gained insight from other referential indices, i.e., the second and third position. By dissociating from a situation (spatially moving it away from you) it is possible to emotionally disconnect from the situation and gain an alternative and more detached perspective. Each of the therapists modelled by Bandler and Grinder also used processes of detachment and dissociation. Satir (1972) used roles work and encouraged her clients to act out the different parts or roles that were present in family units to enable the client to develop more useful strategies of behaviour in response to interpersonal conflict. Perls' gestalt therapy used chairs work as a way of gaining novel solutions to difficult situations. Erickson would introduce empty chairs into the therapy session and he would ask the client to imagine that the chairs represented different members of the family.

Evidence base

There is no empirical evidence that has tested the effectiveness of perceptual positions in resolving interpersonal difficulties. There is increasing evidence that mirror neurons are activated when individuals adopt the kinesics or body movements of other individuals. These studies demonstrate that there is a close relationship between the perceptual and motor systems (Glaser et al 2004). Gallese (2007) has been able to demonstrate that where a person carries out actions, expresses the emotions and experiences the sensations of someone that they observe, their own neural circuits will be activated automatically via the mirror neuron system. This results in the ability to understand another person's mind and Gallese (2007) suggests that this has implications for unconscious communication.

Ramachandran (2009) has studied patients with "anosognosia" a condition where patients who have experienced a stroke and complete paralysis of the left side of their body will completely deny it. They will also completely deny the same condition being present in others even though they can see the paralysis in the other patient. It is assumed from studies into EEG investigations that this is caused by damage to the mirror neurons. Ramachandran (2009) has continued his studies and has been able to demonstrate that mirror neurons are used to process vocal emotions.

Principles of perceptual positions

By adopting the same physiology as another person and specifically mirroring their behaviours you can gain access to understanding their internal state. Once we can represent someone's internal state within ourselves we can begin to pick up clues to the motivation behind their behaviour. This process works by activating a response in the mirror neurons which enable you to imitate the movements of others and read their intentions (Rizzolatti 1999).

Process of perceptual positions

Perceptual positions involves asking a client to adopt three different perspectives: their own or **first position** where they talk about their own perspective, emotions, beliefs and behaviour; the other person's perspective or **second position** where they act as the other person, speak as if they were them, and talk about their emotions, beliefs and behaviour; the detached observer perspective or **third position** where they view things from a dissociated non-emotional perspective and comment on the interaction between the first and second position. By asking the person to adopt the physiology and behaviour of these different perspectives they will gain different clues from each perceptual position. By using different spatial areas, such as chairs, for each of the positions, the client will access an anchored state (described further in chapter 6) that they can neurologically recall each time they return to the specific position.

Procedure

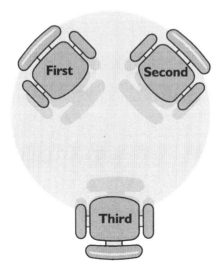

- ಐ The process works best for situations that involve interactions between people

- ಐ Three clear positions are used to gain insight into the different perspectives

- ಐ **First** and **second positions** will be close to each other and placed in the position that they are usually occurring for the individuals concerned

- ಐ **Third position** is placed some way from the first and second position to provide a detached perspective

- ಐ The client talks in first, second and third person language. For example **first position** = *'I, Susan feel this and think this about my situation and Jane's interaction with me'*. **Second position** = *'I, Jane think this and feel this about Susan and her interaction with me.'* **Third position** = *'As a detached observer I notice that Jane and Susan xxxxxxxx'*

- ಐ It is also important that the client breaks state between each position

- ಐ The client will bring their learning and insight from the different perspectives back to the first position and ensure that they are clear about what they need to do to take action.

Exercise

Work with a colleague to consider an interpersonal relationship that has been causing some challenges.

- ಐ Ensure that you are in rapport with your client

- ಐ Help your client to identify the problem that they are having with another person

- ಐ Check their outcome for the exercise and also the ecology of working with this particular issue

- ಐ Position your chairs with the client's guidance

- ಐ Ask the client to sit in first position and describe the problem from their perspective

- As they move to second position ensure that they have broken state with the first position

- Ask the client to sit in second position and describe the problem from this person's perspective

- As they move to third position ensure that they have broken state with the second position

- Ask the client to sit in third position and view things from a detached perspective. What do they think is happening in the relationship? What do they think they could advise the person in first position to do?

- If they have gathered enough information to enable them to gain a different perspective, they can return to first position and determine their next steps

- If they need to gather further information it may be appropriate for them to revisit some or all of the positions before returning finally to first position to determine their next steps.

Applications

Interviews – to prepare for the interview by assessing the likely questions from members of the interview panel. You may also find it helpful following an interview to gain insight into how you came across to other people.

Coaching – as a tool to assist a coachee to gain insight into how other people perceive them.

Management – to resolve interpersonal conflict between two members of staff.

Sports – to model competitors to ascertain behaviours that they are doing that may be useful for the sports person to adopt.

Team Development – to understand motivations of other team members.

Sales – to prepare for sales meetings by understanding what the customer might be seeking and to gain clues to their negotiation process.

HR – as a mediation tool in relationship breakdown such as following disciplinary or grievance processes.

Meta-mirror

The meta-mirror was developed by Robert Dilts (1990) and is an extension of perceptual positions. It is often used when the individual is very emotionally attached to a situation or when there are multiple perspectives to be considered.

Procedure

Sometimes when a client gets to third position in the standard perceptual positions exercise they may experience difficulty in fully dissociating from their emotions and responses to what has been occurring. The meta-mirror can be useful as it uses first, second, third and a fourth position to gain a dissociated view of how the third position relates to the first.

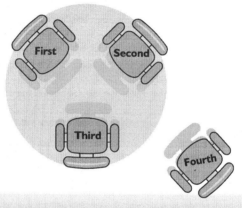

Exercise

- Ensure that you are in rapport with your client
- Help your client to identify the problem that they are having with another person
- Check their outcome for the exercise and also the ecology of working with this particular issue
- Position your chairs for all 4 positions with the client's guidance
- Ask the client to sit in first position and describe the problem from their perspective
- As they move to second position ensure that they have broken state with the first position
- Ask the client to sit in second position and describe the problem from this person's perspective
- As they move to third position ensure that they have broken state with the second position

- Ask the client to sit in third position and view things from a detached perspective. What do they think is happening in the relationship? What do they think of their own behaviour in first position?
- Ask the client to sit in the fourth position ensuring that they have broken state
- Ask the client to take an overview of all three positions. How did their third position relate to their first position?
- Ask the client to step out of fourth position and break state
- Return the client to first position and ask them for their insights and potential actions
- If necessary, return to the other positions to gather further information.

Disney pattern

The Disney Pattern was modelled by Robert Dilts (1994) and emerged from his analysis of Walt Disney's creative process. Dilts was able to identify that Disney used a process of perceptual positions to enable him to bring creativity to his work. These perceptual positions were identified as three aspects of Disney's personality: the dreamer, the realist and the spoiler.

Rationale

Disney used three different perspectives to ensure that his ideas would work on screen, and in business you will find that these processes also occur in enabling an idea to come to fruition.

The Dreamer enabled new ideas and goals to be formed.

The Realist turns the dreamer's ideas into reality.

The Critic is the one who will filter out any ideas that are too ambitious or not believable.

There are many other creativity strategies utilised in a number of different contexts, including a whole series specifically for the business world e.g. Buzan's mind mapping, Brainstorming etc. One model that is similar, in some ways to the Disney strategy, is the Creative Problem Solving strategy of Osborn-Parnes (Parnes 1992).

It uses convergent thinking (i.e. knowledge, decision, evaluation) found in the realist and critic and the divergent thinking (curiosity, inventiveness, activity) found in the dreamer .

Evidence base

A recent action based research study applying the Disney strategy in higher education has demonstrated a 60% improvement in the abilities of students. Pre and post test self assessment questions on levels of creativity, visualisation skills, outcome thinking, problem solving and realisation were utilised and qualitative data supports these findings. The author, Beeden (2009), takes into account the possibility of the effects of autosuggestion and other limitations of the study and proposes that her findings are encouraging with further research recommended in this area.

Principles of Disney strategy

The Dreamer is often the ideas person, or the entrepreneur. This person can come up with the fantastic ideas and may not necessarily know how to turn the ideas into reality. Many ideas of the dreamer never actually happen as the dreamer does not have the thinking patterns to turn them into reality or face obstacles and challenges as they arise.

The Realist is grounded in reality and comes up with a realistic and workable plan or story that will make things happen.

The Critic acts as a filter and will often refine ideas to make them turn into reality. The critic is often detailed in thinking patterns and will usually be able to consider very carefully the consequences of an action or idea.

Process of Disney strategy

Dreamer Position
(Visual Construct)
This position is where you are the visionary, creating possibilities with no constraints.

Realist Position
(Kinaesthetic)
This position is where you take an "as if" frame and think about how it feels and what action needs to happen.

Critic Position
(Visual Recall and Auditory Digital)
A dissociated second view, thinking about where there might be problems. Checking the ecology.

Procedure

⁐ Ensure that you are in rapport with your client

⁐ Identify the area that the client wants to use the strategy for

⁐ Check their outcome for the exercise

⁐ Position your chairs for all 3 positions

⁐ Ask the client to sit in the dreamer position and describe the vision that they have

⁐ As they move to realist position ensure that they have broken state with the dreamer

⁐ Ask the client to sit as the realist and think about what needs to happen to turn the idea into reality

⁐ As they leave this position ensure that they have broken state with the realist position

⁐ Ask the client to sit in the critic position and view where there might be problems

⁐ Return the client to the realist position and agree what steps to take to turn the idea into reality

⁐ If necessary, return to the other positions to gather further information.

Exercise

You can use this process with yourself or a colleague following the steps above.

Ensure that you place out three different positions and that you fully access each of the positions. You may want to use anchoring (described in chapter 6) to ensure that the client accesses specific times when they have experienced the dreamer, the realist and the critic characteristics.

Applications

Project planning – I have used this process with a public health department to facilitate them during a major project plan. We set up 3 different rooms and used props to ensure that the rooms were designed to facilitate thinking from within the three different character roles. The data from each perspective was then collated to agree a concrete action plan that they could move forward with

Marketing – as a tool to assist development of a new brand launch. When this was used with a food production facility the brand experienced a higher than level expected rate of sales.

Teaching – to enable students to think about problem solving strategies.

Team building – as a tool for the team to gain understanding of each others strengths and less developed skills. The team can then work to harness opportunities within the strengths, ensuring that individuals are used to play each of the three roles.

Metaphor

There are many circumstances in life where we use metaphor to help us view things from an alternative perspective. Metaphors communicate directly with our unconscious and can be used with volition to enable a different perspective. We find metaphors in all areas of our life and often do not consider the impact that they have on helping us to gain an alternative viewpoint. Films and TV programmes act as metaphors often providing meaning in abstract ways that enable us to gain a different perspective. When we were growing up fairy stories and nursery rhymes helped us to view things differently. Often tales would involve stories of triumph over adversity. We see metaphors in advertising, in books that we read and in philosophical quotes that are used to present information. Metaphors tap into our subjective meaning and can be used to alter the meaning that we apply to events that happen to us.

Rationale

Metaphors are stories that create symbolic meaning for the unconscious mind of the person experiencing the metaphor. Metaphors tap into the imagination of the individual and enable conceptual thinking. Concepts are often difficult to explain and individuals will use metaphor to portray the conceptual meaning of something when there are insufficient words to fully describe their experience. Metaphors can frequently sum up an entire experience: for the negative gestalt of someone's life e.g. *'my life is like a deck of cards and the whole house has come tumbling down'* or *'one day my ship will come in and I'll be at the airport'*; or for the positive gestalt of life e.g. *'where there is muck there is brass'* or *'every cloud has a silver lining'*. These metaphors will hold many layers of meaning for the speaker, and are easier to portray our mood state than spending time finding words that accurately portray our exact lived experience. Metaphors have been used for centuries from the Bible, fables, fairy stories, legends, folklore, through to psychology and psychoanalysis. In psychology Jung (1964) refers to the use of metaphor and symbology extensively in his discussions on the unconscious mind. He proposes that we use symbolic terms to represent concepts and experiences that we cannot fully understand.

Evidence base

With the development of investigative equipment such as MEG (magneto encephalography), MRI (magnetic resonance imaging), fMRI (functional magnetic resonance imaging), PET (positron emission tomography) it is now possible to measure the relationship between experiences and thinking and emotional processes.

Studies into brain hemisphere processing have suggested that the right brain deals more effectively with metaphors (Beeman et al 1994; Titone 1998). There are also a number of studies which suggest that where the right hemisphere is damaged, there is a reduction in the ability to interpret figurative language (Winner and Gardner, 1977; Hirst, LeDoux and Stein, 1984; Bihrle, Brownell and Powelson, 1986).

There is some evidence of the effective use of metaphor as a visualisation process in conjunction with other approaches in pain management in a Cochrane reviewed randomised control trial (Bowers 1996).

Kazmerski et al (2003) have conducted a study to measure behavioural evidence of metaphor comprehension and present some interesting findings. Individuals with higher levels of IQ are more likely to develop metaphorical meaning compared to individuals with lower IQ scores. They discuss these findings and suggest that this may be influenced by less vocabulary range, reduced working memory and lower ability for comprehension. In measuring meaning making, individuals with higher levels of IQ will automatically seek metaphorical meaning and will find it difficult to reject metaphorically true sentences, whereas they will reject scrambled sentences. In comparing these subjects to individuals with lower IQ levels, the researchers discovered that they were more likely to reject metaphors and scrambled sentences. Conclusions of the study suggest that the results are strongly supportive of a direct model of metaphor processing where figurative meaning is extracted automatically from interaction with the topic and the metaphor used to convey meaning.

Rapp et al (2006) conducted a study that measured processing of metaphoric sentences using fMRI which suggested that other factors might influence hemispheric functioning other than understanding the metaphor.

Cheal (2009) proposes that Metaphor is a promising area for paradox management in organisations. Using metaphors to express and challenge paradoxical thinking is thought to lead to more creativity e.g. *'We really are up the proverbial creek without a paddle'* might be responded to by *'so what kind of boat would you create to steer you through the creek'*.

Principles of metaphor

Metaphor works by providing an opportunity for understanding a particular event or experience through a different mindset. Metaphors can either be simple, e.g. 'as pretty as a picture', or 'as white as a sheet'. They can also be deep or complex with many layers of meaning that enable the unconscious to find experiences and resources to resolve a particular problem or achieve a particular goal. Erickson worked predominantly with metaphor and some excellent examples can be found in *My voice will go with you (Rosen 1992), February Man (Erickson 1989)* and *Hope and Resiliency (Short et al 2005)*. Metaphors work by speaking directly to the unconscious mind and will suggest solutions to problems such that the client finds their own solution to the problem using their existing resources. Metaphors provide an opportunity for reframing of an experience including the opportunity to develop ego strength and the possibility that they can achieve something. Because metaphors involve telling a story about someone or something else, this enables the listener to dissociate from their own experience and view things from a second or third person perspective, or even fourth position where non-human subjects are used within the metaphor.

Process of metaphor

Metaphors can be developed using existing stories that can be adapted to fit specific circumstances or you can make one up. There are a number of elements to consider in designing a metaphor:

- An effective metaphor will change the context of the story while keeping the key relationships the same
- Potential unconscious processes are personified, both abilities and resources and fears and limiting beliefs or blocks
- Parallel learning situations are created that help overcome the problem
- There is a conclusion that involves a celebration or integration of learning.

One example of a metaphor that can be used to gain an alternative perspective and develop ego strength is The Ugly Duckling from Hans Christian Anderson's fairy tale. I have considered this from the case of someone who is depressed and finding it difficult to gain employment.

Reality	The Ugly Duckling	Shared Reality
Depressed and isolated from others	Born small and not part of the flock, looks very different to the other ducklings	*Feeling unwanted, unloved or different*
Having to go out and connect with new people and situations and the anxiety that this provokes	Learning to swim and fly and fear of being left behind as the smallest duckling	*Having to learn new things*
Working with a coach who has got the time to listen to him	Protected by mother swan that can see his qualities. Gets a glimpse of his first view of the swans	*Unconscious process potential*
Being rejected for a number of job applications	Attack in the marsh, winter in the cold pond	*Metaphorical crisis and overcoming hardships*
Achievement at job interview	Ugly duckling sees his transformed image into a swan in his reflection in the water	*Transforming into a higher potential*
Buying a new car or taking a holiday with his wages	The old swans bow before him	*Celebration*

Procedure

There are a number of steps in designing a metaphor.

- ༀ Identify the current problem and the key elements involved in creating the problem
- ༀ Identify the behaviours that are present
- ༀ Identify the preferred outcome
- ༀ Anchor the key elements of the current and outcome state (see anchoring in chapter 6)
- ༀ Choose a context for the story that will be of interest to the other person and be credible
- ༀ Design the story keeping the elements the same to move the person from the present state to the outcome state
- ༀ Change the main characters and experiences in the person's reality within the story
- ༀ Establish new choices and resources within the story, keeping these quite vague so that the person can use their unconscious to find their own resources and solutions
- ༀ Establish a resolution for the characters in the story that leads to the person's outcome state
- ༀ Tell the story using sensory based language
- ༀ Within the story create curiosity and suspense so that they become engaged in the story
- ༀ Leave the person to find their own meaning rather than explain the story.

Exercise

Think of a metaphor that someone has told to you, a book that you have read, or a film that you have watched.

What meaning did this metaphor have for you?

What were the parallel learning's for you from this metaphor?

How did it change your thinking?

Find a colleague to work with and construct a metaphor for them to assist them to gain a different understanding of a particular problem.

Applications

Presentations – think about the aims of your presentation. Where are your audience now and where do you want them to be by the end of the presentation? Construct a metaphor that enables them to move from where they are now to where you want them to be. Tell the metaphor at the beginning of the presentation.

Coaching – to facilitate access of unconscious resources in the client.

Sports – to assist overcome negative or limiting beliefs that are affecting performance.

Sales – to create a story that enables a relationship to the product. Many successful advertisements work with metaphor and can remain powerful for a very long time e.g. the coffee advert that involved a male and female that lived in the same block of flats who borrowed coffee from each other.

Education – as a learning tool to embed unconscious retention and spontaneous recall of key facts. One teacher in the UK won awards following his use of metaphor for teaching 'A' level science students a metaphorical hand dance to recall the key components of cell division.

Reframing

Reframing is the process of changing the way you perceive a situation and so changing its meaning. It works on the principle of separating intention from behaviour where you consider the behaviour and seek out the positive intention rather than a negative one. Eternal optimists spend their life reframing experiences. They automatically look for the positive in a situation and reframe it to apply this meaning to their experience. Pessimists do the opposite. They reframe their life experiences to automatically look for the negative in a situation. Reframing provides you with an alternative perspective to view your experience. There is a bottle of wine containing ½ litre – the pessimist will see it as half empty, the optimist will see it as half full, yet the same bottle of wine is being observed by both people.

Rationale

The first person to write about the systematic utilisation of reframes was Gregory Bateson (1956) who proposed that we get stuck in paradoxical binds that we cannot logic ourselves out of. Watzlawick (1978) refers to Frankl's use of reframing in therapy to enable people to bring meaning back into their lives.

Reframing enables an alternative perspective by dissociating the client from the emotional relationship to the problem state and accessing higher cognitive patterns of thinking.

Evidence base

There is some evidence within cognitive linguistics supported through coaching based reframing interventions such as meta-coaching (Linder-Pelz 2008).

Cheal (2009) in a qualitative study on paradox management in organisations has identified that reframing can be effectively used to apply solutions to problems.

An interesting study analysing dialogue between negotiators and the Davidians during the Waco siege in Texas suggests that reframing during a conflict situation created problems rather than bringing resolution (Agne 2007).

Principles of reframing

Reframing provides the opportunity to gain a third position or meta-perspective on our reality, and thereby gain a more real perspective that may have an alternative meaning. The process changes either the context of where the behaviour is being conducted and gives it an alternative meaning by placing it in another context or it seeks to find the positive intention in the behaviour within the same context.

Process of reframing

Reframing can be conducted by either changing the context – a context reframe, or by changing the content – a meaning reframe.

Context reframes ask the question 'where else would this behaviour be useful?' A meaning reframe asks the question 'what else could this behaviour mean?'

Procedure

Context reframe - works by changing the context of the situation to one where the behaviour would be positive e.g. 'It's too wet to go out for a walk today' to 'The farmers will be pleased, though, they need the rain after the dry spell we have had.' The context of rain has been changed from walking to farming. There are a number of different contexts that can be used such as location, space, frame size, time, duration, circumstances, family, business, age, and resources.

Meaning reframe - This type of reframe works by changing the meaning of the content and is used when someone has made a negative assumption about an event, e.g. 'My husband doesn't buy me flowers; he doesn't love me', to 'It could be that he has noticed how quickly cut flowers deteriorate and so has chosen other ways to show that he loves you'. The meaning of the husband not buying flowers has changed from him not loving her to wanting to demonstrate it in other ways.

Exercise

Look at the following statements and think about how you might provide a reframe for the person who has said the statements.

I am always the last one to leave the office

I end up as a taxi driver all weekend for my kids and don't get any time to myself

I can't persuade my boss to consider me for promotion

Applications

Relationships – to help you think about other reasons why your partner may be behaving in a particular way.

Coaching – to provide alternative suggestions for courses of action.

Sports – to gain insight from situations where the sports person has not performed to their best.

Sales – to provide a contrast frame for the price of something.

Education – to give a rationale and provide motivation for completing a particular piece of course work.

Chapter Six

Changing the Pictures, Sounds and Feelings of How we Think

Time for us to change

WE RESPRESENT our model of the world through our senses using visual, auditory and kinaesthetic input to make sense of our experience. Depending on our filters, outlined in the Communication Model in chapter 2, our internal representation will drive a change in our state. Our state is directly linked to our physiology, e.g. if we feel happy our bodies tend to feel more energised, our eyes are brighter and we have a higher colour to our skin. If we are feeling sad, our bodies tend to feel less energised, our eyes tend to be dull and we usually look paler. This state and resultant physiological change will influence our behaviour which will directly affect our results.

In this chapter I will review three components of NLP that enable us to change how we think and feel:

 **Submodalities, Strategies** and **Anchoring**.

Submodalities

As we have already discovered, we make sense of our world through our neurological system and the 5 senses, representing our reality within representational systems or modalities. A modality is the word used to describe visual, auditory and kinaesthetic systems. What gives experiences meaning is determined by the distinctions you make within a modality, for example, you know the difference between one sound and another because one will be louder, clearer, higher pitched, sound for longer etc. These distinctions are known as submodalities, and they enable us to code, order and give meaning to our experiences. Because submodalities give meaning to our experience if you change the submodalities you can change the meaning of that experience. We are able to choose our submodalities and so we can choose the meaning we make of our experience. Excellence in work is often achieved through being able to make finer and finer distinctions. E.g. a graphic designer or architect will be skilled at making distinctions in their mental pictures, a speech therapist will do so with sound and a dancer will do so with their kinaesthetic system.

Rationale

Dilts (2000) refers to submodalities as first being identified by a French Scientist, Galton, in the 1880's (p.1350). Galton found that each of our mental images consisted of tiny details that gave the imagery meaning. He later was able to demonstrate that the same principle applied to the rest of the senses. William James developed this work and identified preferences in our representations and we also see evidence of this utilisation of finer distinctions in the work of Pavlov – discussed further in this chapter.

Within NLP David Gordon (1978) was the first person to work with submodalities in his metaphor work and we see an extension of this within Lawley and Tompkins Symbolic Modelling (2005).

Erickson frequently worked with submodalities to alter his client's experience of pain or discomfort. As clients recall experiences in their lives, they may recall these as associated or dissociated memories. When a client recalls an experience and views it through his own eyes, as if it were occurring now, he is experiencing the event in an associated form. Clients who can recall an event and view it as if they are watching a movie or picture of themselves are experiencing the event in a dissociated form. By enabling a client to gain greater flexibility in moving between associated and dissociated states, through working with the finer distinctions, the client will be able to make the most appropriate choice for themselves with regard to how they feel about events.

Evidence base

Research into the effectiveness of working with submodalities is probably one of the most widely researched set of techniques within NLP. Much of this work has been in resolving issues such as phobias, post traumatic stress disorder (PTSD) and context specific anxiety disorders.

Koziey et al (1992) used the submodality process of visual-kinaesthetic (V-K) dissociation to demonstrate the effectiveness of neurolinguistic psychotherapy with individuals who experienced anxiety following being raped. Ferguson (1987) and

Hale (1986) both demonstrate the application of NLP and another submodality process, the fast phobia cure, in anxiety related to public speaking. The resolution of a number of different kinds of phobias is evidenced by Allen, (1982), Einspruch and Forman (1985), Kammer et al (1997) and Liberman (1984).

In using general dissociative techniques rather than the specific techniques of fast phobia model and V-K dissociation, Field (1990) has managed to demonstrate effectiveness in working with clients with severe anxiety.

Hossack and Standidge (1993) researched the effectiveness of using generalised imagery and creating coherent meaning by restructuring imagery into a book to relieve depressive symptoms and facilitate goal realisation.

Krugman et al (1985) challenge the effectiveness of NLP as a treatment for public speaking anxiety and suggest that the NLP submodality intervention was no more effective than waiting for an hour.

Dr R Gray (2010) has recently published an article in Traumatology on the effectiveness of the V-K dissociation treatment protocol for the management of PTSD with returning war veterans in the US military. This work supports the NLP Research and Recognition project which is working with the US and Canadian Military on the roll out of a treatment protocol in a researched and clinically managed series of pilot studies - **www.nlprandr.org**.

Gray (2009) has also published his research findings on the use of a range of techniques including submodalities with offenders with various levels of substance use disorders. The results of the programme demonstrated that 30% of participants where abstinent one year following treatment. Additionally participants reported increased positive affect, self efficacy and general satisfaction as a result of the programme. Statistical results show that the NLP interventions were equivalent to those achieved in intensive outpatient care, and were less expensive in time and cost.

Principles of submodalities

Clients who experience all events in an associated form will feel good in any positive experience and will also feel negative in less pleasant experiences. They may feel themselves becoming overwhelmed with emotions at times and may find it difficult to gain an objective perspective on events.

Clients who experience all events in a dissociated form will find it easier to handle more difficult situations and this would also mean that they are not as engaged in positive experiences. Some clients may find that they are associated into negative experiences and remain dissociated from positive experiences.

This can often happen in clients who experience depression, where they have lost joy, meaning and hope in their lives. Other clients may associate into the positive experiences and remain dissociated from the negative. This enables them to distance themselves from negative experiences and fully enjoy positive experiences.

Clients can be supported to develop greater association into experiences through anchoring, described later in the chapter, and also through visualisation. By asking a client to make an internal picture of their experience and then ask them to change the picture so that they are looking through their own eyes, you can assist them to associate into experiences. Equally by asking the client to make a picture of an associated experience that they want to feel less involved with, and then asking them to change the picture so that they can see themselves in the picture can assist dissociation. Further details of submodality processes are available in the writings of Andreas and Andreas (1987).

In goal setting, future desired states are always dissociated which enables maintenance of motivation towards the goal. It is far more compelling to imagine something exciting happening in the future than it is to imagine it having already happened or be in the process of it happening.

Process of submodalities

Submodalities are coded as visual, auditory and kinaesthetic representations and we may have 1, 2 or all 3 senses in play as we experience different inner representations. Some of the submodality distinctions are listed below:

Visual	Auditory	Kinaesthetic
Black & White or Colour	Location	Location
Near or Far	Direction	Size
Bright or Dim	Internal or External	Shape
Location	Loud or Soft	Intensity
Size of Picture	Fast or Slow	Steady
Associated / Dissociated	High or Low Pitch	Movement/Duration
Focused or Defocused	Tonality	Vibration
Changing / Steady Focus	Timbre	Pressure / Heat
Framed or Panoramic	Pauses	Weight
Movie or Still	Cadence	
	Duration	
	Uniqueness of Sound	

For each of these finer submodality distinctions, some of the submodalities will be analogue, i.e. they will be there all of the time and on a continuum, e.g. size is analogical in that something can be infinitely small, infinitely large and anywhere in between. Other submodalities will be digital, i.e. they are either there or not e.g. black and white or colour.

Some submodalities are referred to as critical: they are the ones that provide the meaning of the experience e.g. location might be really important in that if your image of your partner causes a high feeling response if it is positioned on your left, but has a low feeling response if the image is on your right. Within the critical submodalities there will be one submodality that is the driver. If you change this submodality, it will cause the rest of the submodalities to change and the entire meaning of the experience is changed. E.g. changing an image of a bar of chocolate from being very large to very small might be enough to change it from being something that you are almost compulsed to eat to something that you can take or leave.

How to use submodalities

There are a number of techniques within the NLP tools for submodalities, and I have described one of them below. You are advised to experience the remainder of the techniques in a supervised training environment as occasionally you may find that an additional intervention is required, or, on the very rare occasion a client may experience an abreaction.

Mapping across

Mapping Across is a useful technique to use to first understand how submodalities work and second to change the meaning of an experience into something more useful.

The exercise involves eliciting the submodalities of two experiences and then comparing and contrasting them to find out which of them are the same and which are different. You can change the submodalities of one internal representation to the submodalities of another; this is called Mapping Across. If a person wanted to stop eating a particular food you would swap the submodalities of the food they like with a food they dislike. It is inadvisable to do this the other way round and can be dangerous if the person has a food allergy.

Prior to working with someone check that it is totally ok for them to make the change and that they are happy for the change to be permanent.

Procedure

- ෨ Identify the food they like and the food they don't like
- ෨ Elicit the submodalities of each one, using the submodality check list below
- ෨ Identify the critical submodalities, i.e. the differences, and the driver submodality, the one that will make the biggest difference if changed
- ෨ Swap the critical submodalities of the food they like to those of the food they don't like, making sure that you use the driver submodality
- ෨ Test – what do they now think about the food.

Submodalities checklist

Visual

Black & White or Colour?

Near or Far?

Bright or Dim?

Location?

Size of Picture?

Associated /Dissociated

Focused or Defocused?

Focus (Changing/Steady)

Framed or Panoramic?

Movie or Still?

Auditory

Location

Direction

Internal or External?

Loud or Soft?

Fast or Slow?

High or Low? (Pitch)

Tonality

Timbre

Pauses

Cadence

Duration

Uniqueness of Sound

Kinaesthetic

Location		
Size		
Shape		
Intensity		
Steady		
Movement/ Duration		
Vibration		
Pressure/Heat?		
Weight		

Applications

Goal setting – think about a goal that you want to achieve but can't find enough motivation to do it. Make a picture of the goal and then adapt the submodalities until you get a strong motivated feeling towards the goal. (Make sure you are dissociated).

Coaching – work with a client to help them to change the submodalities of a work experience that has been troublesome to them.

Sports – change the submodalities of any internal voices that occur during competitions.

Advertising – I have used this process effectively to adapt advertisements, enabling greater audience involvement by adapting the submodalities in the imagery.

Presentations – understand your own submodalities for how you think about a presentation. If you experience any minor nerves or anxiety, alter your submodalities of your internal pictures, sounds and feelings to see if it makes a difference.

Strategies

As we have already discovered our internal representations provide a direct coding of how we are representing the world to ourselves. We then have finer distinctions that help us to determine things we like compared to things we don't like, our levels of motivation, or how much we like a person. For each behaviour that we do we process information through a sequence of steps that help us achieve a specific outcome. By understanding how we make up our internal representations we can use these to become more effective at selling, competing, relating, managing and motivating.

Rationale

A strategy is a sequence of internal and external representations that consistently achieve a specific outcome or behaviour. We have a strategy for all of our behaviours and these have emerged from habits and patterns of behaviour that we have developed as we grow through time. We continue to do what works regardless of whether it is efficient or not. There are strategies for motivation, procrastination, buying, selling, overeating, exercise, being in a relationship, arguing, loving, making tea, driving the car, learning, winning and losing. We run a strategy for literally everything that we do otherwise we would have to learn something again each time we wanted to repeat it.

When strategies work well they are incredibly effective. It takes little or no effort to run a successful strategy, and when a strategy is not working for us it seems to take an inordinate amount of willpower to change it.

Evidence base

Three randomised control trials have been conducted to test the effectiveness of utilising strategies.

The first study was conducted by Day (1985) with the aim of testing four hypotheses regarding strategy utilisation in a therapy context – total number of subject (n) n= 60. Using the Counsellor Effectiveness Rating Scale, the study demonstrated that the findings were statistically significant for each of the four hypotheses tested, concluding that the client found the therapist credible and having utility.

The second study was conducted by Fremder (1986) to determine whether training visual dot pattern strategies in learning disabled students would transfer to different visual pattern tasks as well as generalize to arithmetic sequencing – n=42. Three groups were set up to receive: standard cognitive strategy training; standard cognitive training plus NLP; a control practice group. The results demonstrated significant transfer effects for both treatment groups when compared to the practice group but no difference between the treatment groups.

The third study elicited the cognitive strategies of excellent performance in intelligent people, with these strategies then being used in a training package. Using pre and post testing there was an improvement in the cognitive strategies group compared to the control group and the exposure group (Malloy et al 1987).

Davis (1984) has demonstrated the effectiveness of mapping strategies for successful and unsuccessful behaviours in 5 individuals who were prelingually deaf. It is unclear which methods were used to demonstrate effectiveness.

Within the sports context Allen (2002) has conducted a single case study of a client who experienced an injury while horse riding. The paper discusses the use of NLP decision strategy redesign amongst other techniques such as EMDR (Eye Movement Desensitisation and Reprocessing) and meditation practices to install a cognitive-behavioural link to enable new skill acquisition. The coach utilised dissociated state rehearsal to install a new strategy.

Skinner and Stephens (2003) have conducted an interesting study measuring the impact of using the preferred representational system of individuals within advertising. Their findings demonstrate that individuals respond best when language is used in adverts that relate directly to their preferred representational system. Where participants used a different representation system, they chose a particular advert based on a different sensory effect. Turan et al (2000) utilised a similar process to determine levels of empathy by matching language. Perceptions of empathy were measured using the Empathetic Understanding Subscale of the Barrett-Lennard Relationship Inventory and findings suggest a significant difference in empathy scores where the interviewer matched the language patterns of the subject.

Swets and Bjork (1990) included NLP in their review of 'New Age' techniques that were being considered by the US army. NLP was one of the techniques considered and the researchers suggest that there is little or no evidence to support the use of such techniques, although they do recommend further study into the effectiveness of mental practice for motor skills.

Principles of strategies

Strategies are understood within the concept of the T.O.T.E model.
The T.O.T.E. model was first introduced in Plans and the Structure of Behaviour published in 1960 by Miller, Galanter and Pribram. T.O.T.E. stands for Test, Operate, Test, and Exit. It is a sequence based on computer modelling where the quality of the data that you receive is based on the quality of the data input. Miller, Galanter and Pribram identified that all complex behaviours are the result of a series of steps that happen as a TOTE model. This behaviour may be conscious or usually unconscious. Bandler and Grinder noticed that although individuals used a preferred representational system, individuals consistently followed a specific sequence to enable decision making, learning, and behaviours (1980).

The key parts of a strategy within the TOTE model are the representational systems that are accessed and the outcome achieved by accessing the representational systems in a particular order or sequence. In order to understand strategies it is useful to pay attention to the elements of the strategy which are the representational systems used, and the sequence which is the order in which they are run to achieve a particular outcome, useful or not useful. Over time we may find that we have outgrown the usefulness of some of our strategies. By understanding the elements and sequence we can change or redesign a strategy, specifically tailored to the desired outcome, for others and ourselves. We can also find out how successful people run their strategies and model these for our own use.

Process of working with strategies

In eliciting strategies it is important to notice both the conscious and unconscious steps that the individual takes to run the strategy. There are a number of clues to pay attention to that will give you an indication of the components and sequence of a strategy. These clues may occur simultaneously or separately.

Verbal language identified through representational systems and predicates

- ∞ Body language that can back up or reinforce eye accessing cues
- ∞ Eye accessing cues that can back up the verbal and body language
- ∞ Synaesthesia where there is an automatic link between one representational system and another e.g. it grabbed my eye – is a link between kinaesthetic (grabbed) and visual (eye).

Procedure

Initially, it is easiest to elicit a *buying strategy*. When you elicit a buying strategy, it is important to check a number of things so that you get a clear strategy

- ∞ Is the person happy with the purchase?
- ∞ Were they alone when they bought it? - if not, you may get somebody else's strategy. Was the purchase just for themselves – if it was for someone else you may get a different strategy?
- ∞ Can they recall it clearly?

There are a number of things to take into account when you elicit the strategy.

- ∞ The person should be able to access the time when they made the purchase and experience it as if it were happening now

∞ You can anchor the state (described in the next section) to enable them to recall the state clearly

∞ Speak in the present tense

∞ Use all accessing cues: predicates, eyes, breathing, tonality, gestures

∞ Ask open questions e.g. *How do you decide, know, think, etc. to . . . ?*

∞ Use unspecified predicates e.g. *how did you know?*

∞ Give more than one option e.g. *did you try on one or more pairs of shoes?*

∞ Backtrack to get to the next step if further detail is required. E.g. if they have told you that they are paying for their purchase, and you want to find out what process they went through in the changing room, you will need to backtrack to the beginning and ask them to talk you through their process again

∞ Make sure that you get a logical sequence. If there are any clearly missing pieces, ask them further questions

∞ Notice loops or recurrent sequences of steps where the person is repeating steps a number of times, e.g. trying on several different types of shoe and walking up and down in them

∞ Make sure that you have all the key functional pieces (the initial test or trigger that starts the strategy, the operate, the test and the exit) in the major representational systems, which will be required as you utilise the strategy.

Exercise

Work with a colleague to identify their decision making strategy for a recent purchase

Identify the key elements of their representational systems and the order in which they use them

Feedback their strategy by offering them an alternative item to purchase.

An example of how to do this is given on the following page.

Cont'd

'I saw the shoes, they looked really comfortable. I tried them on, loved them and asked the price. I paid the assistant'

I saw the shoes – **Visual V**

They looked really comfortable – **Visual/Kinaesthetic V/K**

I tried them on – **Kinaesthetic K**

Loved them – **Kinaesthetic K**

Asked the price – **auditory and auditory digital A/Ad**

I paid the assistant – **auditory digital Ad**

So, the strategy is **V** → **V/K** → **K** → **A/Ad** → **Ad**

Alternative purchase offered to them – a new notebook.

Look at this notebook – **visual**

See how it feels – **visual/kinaesthetic**

Feel the leather – **kinaesthetic**

Speak to me about any questions you might have – **auditory/ auditory digital**

Further information on price and specification is here if you require it – **auditory digital**

Applications

Learning – Identify your own successful learning strategy in one context and map this across to a subject that you find less easy to learn.

Selling – Eliciting the decision making strategy for purchase is an effective tool in the sales process. Remember to use rapport and be clear that the outcome is a win: win.

Sports – Coaches can work with sports enthusiasts to elicit the motivation strategy for one sport and transfer this to another sport that they are less enthusiastic about. A colleague was competing in a triathlon and was always motivated for the bicycle and running elements, and always managed to find excuses for avoiding swimming training. He found out his strategy for motivation for the first two exercises and used this to create a compelling motivation for swimming.

Relationships – Some relationships flounder because couples do not understand each others strategy for being in a relationship. In my own relationship I need to **hear** that I am loved whereas my husband needs to **feel** that he is loved. We have learnt to give each other evidence of being loved in the most relevant system.

Anchoring

The NLP Communication Model assumes that our state gives rise to our behaviour. If we are in a negative state we will often react with less than useful behaviours and if we are in a positive state, our behaviours are usually more useful. Our state results from a combination of mental and physical processes and will affect how we relate to others and how we might perform in a given context. Our state also directly affects how we filter information. It is possible to select states for specific contexts e.g. if we want to feel motivated, we can recall times in the past when we have felt motivated and anchor that state to now. We can also remove negative states by collapsing them into positive states.

Rationale

An anchor is a stimulus response that is applied to a state. Anchoring enables you to select and access internal states. Each state accessed will be associated with the total context in which it occurred, both the internal and external conditions, what you were doing, what you were thinking and so on. Anchors are any stimulus that takes us back to a specific time and place: e.g. a song can often bring us back to a place and time with which we associate it and reactivate an entire memory as an experience in the here and now. Our memories are set up so that there is a connection between the context and the associated state. An anchor may be a sensory input (Visual, Auditory, Kinaesthetic, Olfactory or Gustatory) that was part of the original experience. It can also be a word – perhaps the label that we have given to the state.

Evidence base

There are 3 studies that look at the effectiveness of anchoring in the field of therapy, and 1 study in education.

Field (1990) used a combination of NLP techniques including anchoring and reports the single case study findings of a client with severe anxiety. Anchoring was used in the first session to access inner resources that existed for the client, these were 'superimposed' over the anxiety state.

In a control trial, Brandis (1986) was able to demonstrate some change in parents with anger towards their children in a process that used collapse anchors: however, the study findings suggest that the self-anchoring process was more useful than the collapse anchors process.

Gray (2009) has utilised anchoring in his research with offenders with various levels of substance use disorders. Participants on the programme were taught to anchor several predefined states which where then enhanced to ecstatic states, as a series of resource states that could be accessed when required. Over time the participants in the study integrated the anchors into single state labelled 'Now'. Gray suggests that this state creates a basic felt experience of Jung's deep Self which was then associated to well formed and meaningful outcomes. His findings demonstrated that 30% of participants where abstinent one year following treatment. Additionally participants reported increased positive affect, self efficacy and general satisfaction as a result of the programme. Statistical results show that the NLP interventions were equivalent to those achieved in intensive outpatient care, and were less expensive in time and cost.

Squirrel (2009) utilised anchoring in her work with young children displaying social, emotional and behavioural difficulties. Anchors were applied when the children had a success, and the anchor was also fired when the child experienced difficulties to add a resource state to the current situation. Findings of her experimental study suggest that some NLP techniques are useful with this group and in comparing the trial group to the control group, there was an improvement in behaviour.

Principles of anchoring

Anchoring or stimulus response is based on classic conditioning theory (Pavlov 1904/1927). Pavlov has studied the work of Twitmeyer (1902) who identified the hammer – knee jerk response. In his experiments, physiologist Pavlov demonstrated that dogs have a salivary reflex that could be conditioned to unnatural stimuli such as ringing a buzzer and that where this stimuli is linked to the dog's food, the dog would develop an associated response between the stimuli of the buzzer and food, even when the food was not shown. He was also able to demonstrate how conditioned responses could also be eliminated using a similar process. Operant conditioning (Skinner 1938) extended the early theory and states that individuals will generalise on behavioural responses in situations which are similar to the original one where the conditioned response was developed. He developed his theory further to include negative reinforcement or escape learning where we remove or avoid something unpleasant. This is supported by the work of Adler (1927/1992) and Pert (1997). Damasio (1994) identified that conditioning involves excitation of neurons which hold a neural memory in response to the impulse, resulting in the release of neurotransmitters and activation of the next neuron, and hence activation of the entire neurological chain, leading to a behavioural response.

Process of anchoring

There are a number of essential elements that are required for an anchor to work.

- Intensity of the experience. The anchor will be more effective if the person recalls the most intense experience of the state. For the best result an anchor should be created when the experience is at its most intense.

- Timing of the anchor. The anchor is applied just before the state reaches its peak and released as soon as it has reached its peak.

- Uniqueness of the stimulus. The anchor should be something that is unlikely to be triggered when it is not wanted as an anchor. Using a handshake, for example, as an anchor for creativity may be triggered every time your hand was shaken, not only when you wished to access the creative state. There are certain locations that might be useful such as a knuckle or ear-lobe (somewhere that is unlikely to get triggered accidentally).

- Replication of the stimulus. Topping up or stacking the anchor from time to time will maintain and increase its power.

- Number of times. Applying the anchor several times when you are setting the anchor will increase its power.

Procedure

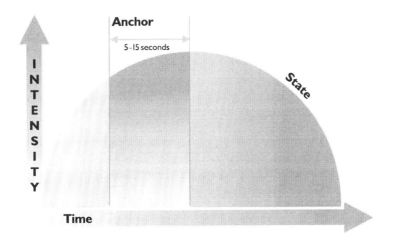

- ৩০ Be in rapport with your client

- ৩০ Identify the outcome with the client and decide on the state that they require

- ৩০ Identify the location of the anchor. When applying a physical anchor it is important to get permission to touch the other person and also to ensure that you are in rapport with them.

- ৩০ Get into the state you are eliciting and ask the client to recall a specific time when they were in that state. Ensure that the client is in an associated and intense state.

- ৩০ Anchor the state by touching the client in a specific location (knuckles are usually effective and also appropriate to touch). Apply the anchor when the state is at its most intense. Utilising sensory acuity to calibrate the change in state of the client will assist you to ensure that the client is in the most intense state when you apply the anchor.

- ৩০ Break state by asking the client to think of something else e.g. what they had for breakfast

- ৩০ Test the anchor by firing it. Distract the client by asking another question and then fire the anchor and notice the response, using your sensory acuity.

There are two other processes within anchoring: collapse anchors and chaining anchors.

Collapsing anchors is a useful technique to use when a client habitually responds in an unresourceful way to a particular situation and enables the client to have more positive states in that situation. It is particularly useful when the client is operating an away from motivation pattern and wishes to change it to a towards motivation response, e.g. moving from a fear response to an accepting, happy or calm response. The process is similar to that of setting a resource anchor with an added component of collapsing the negative state into the positive one.

Chaining anchors is a technique that can be used when the gap between the present state and the desired state is large. The process works by using a series of intermediate states to move the person's neurology from the present state to the desired state in small steps rather than one leap.

Exercise

Work with a client to anchor a specific state following the steps outlined opposite.

Alternatively, you may want to think about a particular situation where you would benefit from additional resources. Work with a colleague to anchor these states for yourself.

Applications

Selling – Use triggered responses to anchor clients to your products. Some of the anchors that have worked very well in the past have been advertisements that have included a catch phrase or a particular piece of music. The majority of people will be able to complete the slogan *'Clunk Click . . . . . .'* or *'A mars a day . . . .'.*

Presenting – Following a presentation when the previous speaker has not gone down well usually means that your presentation receives an equally poor or only marginally better reception. Change your position by ensuring that you stand in a different location: in this way you avoid firing the negative anchor of the last speaker's slot.

Sports – Many athletes and sports people have an anchored movement that they use when they win. This can also be used at other times to access the resourceful state and maintain motivation to win.

Teaching – We anchor different things to different parts of the room. Future learning we place on the right of the room as you look to the front which accesses Construct eye patterns, past learning and negative states we anchor to the left side of the room, accessing generalised Recall eye patterns. We also use set pieces of music to bring the group back into class at the end of break-times.

Confidence – Some people have lucky ties, lipstick, socks, perfumes, pants. All of these act as anchors and on a day when you are feeling less confident, you can access additional confidence and resources by wearing your lucky socks!

Chapter Seven

Change Management

Time to make a change

AS WE are already beginning to discover NLP is a powerful tool that can be used to facilitate change in ourselves and other people. Once we identify the internal thinking processes, feelings and emotional states that people use and the behaviours that result from our thoughts and feelings, we open up the possibility of change to enable us to achieve our goals.

Change within organisations, teams or individuals can happen at many different levels, from small step change to massive cultural change. By taking responsibility for managing the change it is possible to achieve effective outcomes and also to make the smallest amount of change for the greatest benefit.

Any change agent needs to consider which intervention will bring about the most effective and sustained change.

Logical levels of change

The work of Gregory Bateson (1972/2000) has influenced many of the current thinkers in organisational and individual change. His systemic perspective on change and individual growth and development inspired the concepts of NLP, Learning Organisation and Accelerated Learning. Robert Dilts (1990) also developed his model of Logical Levels of Change from Bateson's work. It outlines the levels at which change can take place. Dilts concluded that in order to bring about change you needed to work at the level above that at which the problem lies.

Logical levels provide an invaluable tool for planning, implementing and evaluating any change programme. It is particularly useful in considering whether all the levels are aligned to bring about true and congruent change. For example some organisations have inspirational mission statements and yet the actions of its people do not reflect the mission. Logical levels can help you understand why this happens and how you can work to align all the levels

Rationale

Logical levels of change is based in systems theory. Bateson was fascinated by the categorisation process that individuals use to make sense of their experiences and suggested a series of generalisations through which individual development, growth and potential can be understood (2000 p. 177 – 193). In summary his theory proposes that we observe the signals of others and interpret these by making finer and finer discriminations to seek implicit meaning. The interpretation that we make from this information acts as a feedback loop, to enable us to gain insight into our own behaviour, which we will then adapt to facilitate ongoing communication and understanding of ourselves and others. Dilts has adapted Bateson's work and provided discrimination across six different levels of abstraction from our external environment through to our mission or purpose in life.

Evidence base

Qualitative evidence suggests that it has a place in coaching and can foster insight and awareness of leadership skills and attributes in a number of different contexts including Financial Services (Wales 2002), and the Health Service (Clark 2008). Sullivan (2002) also discusses a case study report providing qualitative evidence of its effectiveness as a model in facilitating value-driven change management in organisations. This is supported by Cheal's (2009) qualitative study into the management of Organisational Paradox. Cheal suggests that Dilts' model is a useful model for separating out the various layers of an organisation to understand the paradoxes.

The model has also been used as a qualitative research tool by Walton et al (2009) to gather data that enabled understanding of the meaning, nature and benefits of exercise for women moving into their middle years.

Principles of logical levels

Logical levels of change was developed by Dilts (1990) as an extension of his understanding of Bateson's systems theory. Dilts proposes that there are

3 systemic models of change: Logical levels of *change* which assumes that in learning, change and communication there are natural hierarchies; logical levels of *thinking*; and, *neurological* levels. For the purposes of change management, we will consider logical levels of change.

Each of the levels describes the attributes, thinking and behaviour that is evident within this level of abstraction. Each of the higher levels influences the levels beneath it, and if you change higher levels of abstraction you will always influence the lower levels. However, if you change the lower levels, you will not necessarily influence the higher levels.

- ❧ Mission - As an organisation, a team or an individual you are part of a larger system. At this level you can consider the impact of change on that system. For example, an organisation may want to think about its role in its local community, or on the global community.

- ❧ Identity - This level has to do with how we think about our sense of self. It is about who we are. With an organisation or team it will be about the identity it portrays and what it considers as it's unique nature.

- **Beliefs / Values** - Beliefs are things that we hold to be true and are about why we do the things we do. For example, a person with a belief that it is important to be on time for an appointment will act differently from someone who believes that the time of an appointment is a guideline.

  Values are those things that the individual or organisation hold to be important. An organisation which values employee safety above speed of production will be different from the one that has those values the other way round. The key to alignment of values is the similarities between espoused values and values in action.

- **Capabilities** - This is about how you do things. It is about the skills, qualities and strategies that you use. Implementing any change will usually require a change in your competencies.

- **Behaviour** - This is about what you do, about your physical actions. It is important to remember here one of the presuppositions of NLP *that a person is not their behaviour.* In any change work it is important to separate a person's behaviour from their identity.

- **Environment** - This level concerns the external conditions to which you react. It will include things such as the place you work in, your team members, customers, your home etc.

Process of logical levels

The language that individuals use will communicate at which level of abstraction they are thinking. The same process applies in organisations. By listening carefully to the language being used you can become aware of the amount of alignment that exists within organisations. I have given two separate examples below. Each example highlights the differences between aligned and misaligned thinking, the first for an individual and the second one for an organisation. I have then suggested the level of change at which to intervene (i.e. the one above the misaligned level) and the proposed intervention.

Individual

Level	Aligned thinking	Misaligned thinking
Mission	My purpose in life is create a fairer and more equal society	My purpose in life is to create a fairer and more equal society
Identity	I am a manager of an organisation that deals with issues of social responsibility	I am a manager of an organisation that deals with issues of social responsibility
Values/Beliefs	**I believe that all people are equally important and should receive the same level of support**	*I believe that I have worked hard to get where I am and that if everyone took the same opportunity and approach, they could be just as successful*
Capabilities	I communicate effectively with others **and I listen carefully to ensure that I incorporate all views in my decision making**	I communicate effectively with others
Behaviours	**I use reflective listening in my discussion with others**	*I make sure that people know that they can approach me*
Environment	I live in an environment that enables me to minimise waste and use public transport for my journeys	I live in an environment that enables me to minimise waste and use public transport for my journeys

The misalignment is occurring at value and belief level, which leads to incongruent capabilities and behaviours, therefore the intervention will be offered at identity level. I would coach the individual to help me to understand their meaning of social responsibility and how they perceive their role in ensuring that this is also carried through the organisation. On gathering this information, I would anticipate that I would be able to work with the individual, possibly using perceptual positions discussed in chapter 5, to assist them to gain insight into the impact of their approach and current value and belief set on others.

Organisational

Level	Aligned thinking	Misaligned thinking
Mission	Our purpose is to be the largest producer of branded goods in Europe	Our purpose is to be the largest producer of branded goods in Europe
Identity	I am a Senior Manager	I am a Senior Manager
Values/Beliefs	We are committed to fair and transparent employment practices. I believe in the potential of all and the impact that a motivated workforce can have on productivity	We are committed to fair and transparent employment practices. I believe in the potential of all and the impact that a motivated workforce can have on productivity
Capabilities	**I am flexible and creative in my thinking and work well with others to gain their views and input. I prefer a team based approach to problem solving**	*I write regular monthly reports that demonstrate how I have used a creative approach to bring cost pressures down*
Behaviours	**I have an open door policy and use regular team briefings to gather feedback and ideas**	*My team know that they can speak to me if they need to*
Environment	**My desk is situated in an open plan office**	*I often work from home because the open plan office stops me from thinking clearly*

This misalignment is occurring at capability level and it may be that the manager is unaware of the impact of their current communication style on others. It may also be that through coaching I would gain further insight into their values and be able to use these in reframing (chapter 5) how they currently communicate to facilitate a different behavioural response.

Procedure

There are specific questions that you can ask to find out how aligned someone is in their logical levels.

Individual

-   Mission - What is your purpose in business/life? For some people their mission is quite small and they may not be able to answer questions about their purpose in life. Sometimes it helps to ask them who they relate to, or in which sectors do they work.

-   Identity – Who are you? This can be just one *I am* statement, or may be several. For some individuals who are unclear about who they are, you may want to ask them who are they are not that they would like to be, e.g. *Is there anyone else that you would like to be or that you particularly admire and would want to be like?*

-   Beliefs / Values - What do you believe is true about you and those around you that enables you to do what you do? What beliefs do you hold about yourself? What beliefs would you like to hold that are not currently present?
  What is important to you about what you do? What factors influence your decisions?

-   Capabilities - What are your key capabilities? For some people they may prefer to answer the question *what are your key skills and competencies.* What skills do you not have yet that would enable you to be who you are or who you want to be?

-   Behaviour - What do you do? How do your behaviours reflect you? What behaviour do you have that you prefer not to have?

-   Environment - Where do you work? What are the external influences in your life and on you? Where do you not work that you would like to work?

Organisational

-   Mission - What is the organisation's purpose in business? This is different from their mission statement. Sometimes it helps to ask them who their key stakeholders are.

-   Identity – Who are you? Who is the organisation? Who does the organisation see itself as?

ஐ Beliefs / Values - What does the organisation believe is true about itself and its employees that enables it to achieve it's mission? What beliefs would the organisation like to hold that are not currently present? What is important to the organisation about what it does? What factors influence its decision making?

ஐ Capabilities - What are the organisation's key capabilities, skills and competencies? What skills does it not have yet that would enable it to be who it sees itself as?

ஐ Behaviour - What does the organisation do? How do the behaviours within the organisation reflect it? What behaviours are present that the organisation would prefer not to see and would want to stop, get rid of or change?

ஐ Environment - Where does the organisation work? What are the external influences on the organisation? Where does the organisation not work or cover that it would like to?

Exercise

Summarised here is an exercise that can be useful in helping you gain insight into a change that you have made at work recently.

ஐ What change did you make to your external environment?

ஐ What changes did you make to your behaviour?

ஐ What changes did you make to how you approach things? Were there any skills that enabled you to make the change? Were there any skills that you were required to learn to make the change?

ஐ What changes did you make about what you believed to be true? What was important to you about the change?

ஐ What difference has the change made to the way you think about yourself?

ஐ How did this change alter how you are part of the larger system? How did this change effect how you think about your purpose in life?

Now as you look back at your answers, which level of change had the greatest impact on your results?

Applications

Management – The process can be used to help you gain understanding of why a department may not be functioning as effectively as it could. I have utilised this process to understand and support the management of a small department of a major organisation that had gone through radical change in the last few years. The department was the only one that had not moved premises and was still being managed by the same manager. It had not experienced any of the major change that the rest of the organisation had experienced and was getting left behind. It was causing major frustration for the Head Office as it seemed to refuse to move with the times. Using this model it was clear that the department had lost touch with the mission of the organisation. It took only a small step to help the staff to see where the organisation was going for them to come on board and feel involved and contributing.

Selling – Some individuals will buy an item at behavioural level and others will buy at identity or even mission level. Cars are a good example. For some, a car is a functional item that enables them to move from a to b in a timely and efficient manner – the car holds meaning at behaviour and capability level. For others a car is a status symbol or says something about the person's identity – the car holds meaning at value or identity level. Selling the perceived style and status of a car to someone who views them at behaviour level would potentially switch off the buyer.

Coaching – The model provides an excellent coaching tool to enable someone to understand their motivations for applying for a particular job. It can also be used to ascertain levels of alignment in the coachee's thinking if they are experiencing challenges in achieving their goals.

Conflict management and negotiation– Helping each side to see the respective levels of meaning of the other party can often be a major step forward in negotiations or conflict situations.

The SCORE model of change

Many NLP techniques require a number of steps to determine if the intervention is appropriate and they also follow a similar structure. The structure involves understanding the problem state and how this is represented by the individual, the underlying cause of the problem, the preferred outcome, any resources that the client may bring into play to resolve the problem, and the consequences or effect of the intervention. By using the SCORE model it is possible to determine the main elements of change to identify the most appropriate place to offer an intervention.

Rationale

Dilts (2000 p. 1173) suggests that it is possible to work with problems using the unified field theory. By understanding the nature of the problem at the different logical levels, different time frames such as past, present or future, and different perspectives such as first, second and third position, it is possible to offer the most appropriate intervention.

Evidence base

There is no empirical evidence base to support the effectiveness of SCORE as a model. Techniques that use SCORE such as anchoring, fast phobia cure, V-K dissociation are all evidenced and discussed in chapter 6.

Principles of SCORE

The S.C.O.R.E. model identifies the primary components necessary for effectively organising information about any goal or change. By understanding each of the elements required for change it becomes possible to determine where to make the intervention.

The letters stand for **S**ymptoms, **C**auses, **O**utcome, **R**esources, and **E**ffects. These elements represent the minimum amount of information that needs to be gathered to create changes.

- ✖ Symptoms are typically the most noticeable and conscious aspects of the presenting problem or present state. It may be that the individual is constantly late for work, or that the organisation fails to meet financial targets.

- ✖ Causes are the underlying elements responsible for creating and maintaining the symptoms. They are usually less obvious than the symptoms themselves. Lateness may be caused by the bus route changing, or a marital breakdown that has resulted in child care difficulties. Failure to meet financial targets may be caused by an increase in raw material costs, or by poor financial management.

- ✖ The Outcome is the actual goal or desired state that would take the place of the symptoms. To manage working hours in an honest and reliable manner, or to reduce costs over time to bring the business back in budget within 6 months.

- **Resources** are the underlying elements responsible for creating and maintaining the outcome. Time management may require organising ride-sharing or flexible working hours. Financial management may require skills from another team to assist to address a difficult period or may require negotiation with a supplier to reduce costs. There are some techniques, such as reframing and anchoring, which can be used for applying particular resources.

- **Effects** are the results of or responses to the achievement of a particular outcome. Often the desired effect of achieving an outcome is mistaken for the outcome itself. Positive effects are often the reason or motivation for wanting the outcome to begin with. Negative effects can create resistance or ecological problems and the person may find it easier to not change. The effect might be to reduce working hours each week so that child care can be managed, or it may be that managing spiralling costs more effectively may allow for longer term investment within the next 2 years.

Understanding SCORE

Process of SCORE

Each of the elements above is considered along with certain characteristics of features that are present. These include:

- Vital signs associated with each of the steps above. Vital signs include factors such as eye accessing cues, representational systems, body postures and gestures, critical submodalities, motivational patterns such as those found in metaprogrammes (chapter 10), criteria or values (chapter 10) and beliefs

- Behavioural demonstration of the elements. How does/would somebody behave at each of the points within the SCORE model?

- Levels of change including behaviours, capabilities, beliefs and identity.

Procedure

The procedure involves laying out each of the elements and considering the vital signs, behavioural demonstration and levels of change.

Representation	Symptom Problem state	Cause Present state	Outcome Desired State	Resources Techniques	Effect Results
Vital Signs eye accessing cues, representational systems, body postures/ gestures, critical submodalities, metaprogrammes criteria or values					
Behaviours					
Capability					
Beliefs					
Identity					

I have laid out the representation from the 2 scenarios given earlier: poor time management and financial pressure.

Poor time management

	Symptom	Cause	Outcome	Resources	Effect
	Problem state	Present state	Desired State	Techniques	Results
Representation	Consistently late for work	Change in bus timetable	To work the current number of hours and to have good timekeeping	Possibility of ride-share or change of working times	Motivated and committed employee doing the required number of hours
Vital Signs eye accessing cues, representational systems, body postures/ gestures, critical submodalities, metaprogrammes criteria or values	Comes in, rushed, harassed, avoids eye contact. Speaks in fast visual language. Submodalities are unable to be elicited because they are in a negative state. Metaprogrammes are driven by sort for others, perceiver and external frame of reference (see chapter 10) Values are predominantly home based and major value driver is work life balance as an 'away from' (see chapter 10)	Eyes accessing and representational system is kinaesthetic. Metaprogrammes as in problem state. Values as in problem state	Eye accessing and representational system is auditory digital and visual construct	Eye accessing and representational system is auditory digital and visual construct. Metaprogramme and values remain unchanged	Eye accessing visual construct. Representational system positive kinaesthetic. Metaprogrammes remain unchanged

	Symptom	Cause	Outcome	Resources	Effect
	Problem state	Present state	Desired State	Techniques	Results
Behaviours	Rushing. Avoiding speaking to people Work is completed in an untidy manner	Seeking alternative ways to get to work as the buses run erratically and need to fit around child minder times	Relaxed employee working the correct number of hours on flexi time	Communication to the organisation to ascertain if there is the possibility of a ride-share	Employee works for the required number of hours and productivity and effectiveness increases
Capability	Messy work Poor communication skills	Demonstrated commitment and loyalty to retain job	Improved timekeeping	Communication and relationship building across the organisation	Desire to learn new skills
Beliefs	Believes that she is not good at her job and is also a poor mother	Believes that keeping her job is important so that she can give a good quality of life to her children	Work is important and that she can contribute to the organisation	Work is a caring organisation and is helpful to it's employees	That she can contribute more
Identity	I am bad	I can't be a good mum and be a good employee	I am good at what I do	I am a valued member of the company	I am a valued member of the company

Financial pressure on the business

	Symptom	Cause	Outcome	Resources	Effect
	Problem state	Present state	Desired State	Techniques	Results
Representation	Costs spiralling out of control	Increased raw material costs	Costs in control	Excellent negotiation skills in procurement	Opportunity to invest longer term
Vital Signs eye accessing cues, representational systems, body postures/ gestures, critical submodalities, metaprogrammes criteria or values	5% loss each month on the bottom line that is cumulative. Metaprogrammes resulting in high Judger drive from the Board and procedural thinking (see chapter 10) Values of 'away from' having to survive (see chapter 10)	Increase in raw material cost by 8% Metaprogrammes of procedural, away from, detail. Values of 'away from' having to survive (see chapter 10)	Raw material price negotiated downwards. Bottom line growth of 1.5% per month that is cumulative. Metaprogrammes of 'towards' growth and new business development	Positive kinaesthetic and visual construct in procurement department who are keen to manage the raw materials price. Metaprogrammes of towards. Values of efficiency and effectiveness	Positive kinaesthetic and visual construct. Potential investment asset of 12% by year end

	Symptom	Cause	Outcome	Resources	Effect
	Problem state	Present state	Desired State	Techniques	Results
Behaviours	Panic. Cost cutting. Job shedding	Realism. Communication amongst the team	Commence discussions for new business developments	Proactive, extension of procurement role into other areas in the business	Increased efficiency savings
Capability	Ability to manage under pressure	Effective communication. Strategic thinking	Strategic thinking, Creativity	Communication and relationship building across the organisation	Increased performance capability
Beliefs	Belief that the business is failing	Belief that if we don't do something we will fail	Belief that the business has good potential if it can manage costs	Belief in the potential of cross functional working	Greater corporate cohesion and effective organisational working
Identity	We are failures	We might be good enough to pull this off	We are a great team	All functions contribute well to the business	We are successful

Exercise

Think about an area of your life that you would like to change. Referring back to the examples given above, complete the table below.

Notice where you think you can make the change to have the most amount of benefit.

Symptom	Cause	Outcome	Resources	Effect
Problem state	Present state	Desired State	Techniques	Results
Representation				
Vital Signs eye accessing cues, representational systems, body postures/ gestures, critical submodalities, metaprogrammes criteria or values				
Behaviours				
Capability				
Beliefs				
Identity				

Applications

Management – As a diagnostic tool to identify the key areas that can be addressed as levers for change.

Relationships – This can be a helpful model in assisting you to identify the real cause in a particular situation rather than the symptom. This then leads to you identifying existing resources that you can access to help you move towards your outcome.

Coaching – This can be used as a coaching tool to identify areas of influence that the coachee has and also to determine next steps.

Be the change you want
to be in the world.

Mahatma Gandhi.

Chapter Eight

The Language of NLP

Time to communicate

LANGUAGE IS the process by which we communicate our experience of the world to others. We also use language internally, our internal dialogue, to help us make sense of our subjective experience. We use language to bring people closer towards us and we use language to move people away from us. Language is our verbal reasoning and provides a representation of our internal experience.

By understanding our own linguistic representation of our world we can gain greater insight into how we think and how we communicate our model to other people. We can also use the same process to understand others. Once we understand how someone else is thinking we are presented with the opportunity to assist them to change how they think, which will directly influence their results.

There are many language patterns within NLP and it was one of the first components modelled by Bandler and Grinder and produced in their writings, *Structure of Magic: Volumes I and II*. In this section I will cover some of the main linguistic elements of NLP:

Metamodel, Milton Model, Linguistic Presuppositions and **Hierarchy of Ideas**.

There are other advanced language techniques that are taught in NLP, many of which are covered at Master Practitioner level. The majority of these are based on the structure of the language patterns as they are laid out in this chapter.

Metamodel

In developing NLP Bandler and Grinder started by identifying the language patterns of Virginia Satir and Fritz Perls. These psychotherapists achieved their remarkable results by taking the client from the abstract to the specific. From this the Meta Model was devised. The purpose of the Meta Model is to help people recover some of the information that they had deleted, distorted or generalised in order to have formed their current internal representations. It can also be used to get people to be more specific or take them out of trance, where their attention is fixed on something specific and is preventing them looking at other possible solutions. By recovering the information you can help someone find more choices either at a behavioural level or at a conceptual or experiential level.

Rationale

Meta means something of a higher or second-order kind. In this instance it is a model of language that is used to describe or analyse another person's model of the world. People delete, distort and generalise their experience in order to make sense of it and communicate it to others. Following this 'filtering' process we only get a Surface Structure representation of their experience. The Meta Model helps us to recover the unconscious meaning and experience of someone else's world, i.e. the Deep Structure.

Evidence base

Doemland (2001) has conducted an empirical research study to examine the relationship between an athlete's cognitive model of performance and their results. The study looked at the use of language by the athletes and how this related to their athletic achievement. Findings suggest that ranked athletes generated a statistically significant number of well formed goal statements than non ranked athletes. The study also included qualitative analysis of the meta model violations, the deletions, distortions and generalisations that were being used. Findings also suggest that where these were present they had a varied effect on how the athlete verbally expressed their perception of their performance.

Sandhu (1991) presents a conceptual map of using the meta model as one of the tools in enabling clients to access their deep structure of their subjective experience to change beliefs about existing behaviour. Forman (1986) also presents a similar conceptual map as an approach in couple's therapy.

Cheal (2009) suggests that awareness of and denominalisation of Paradox within organisations can be useful, particularly where there is no shared definition e.g. Leadership: 'how are people leading', 'what specifically do you mean by leadership'?

Principles of the meta model

The Meta Model is specifically designed to recover the distortions, deletions and generalisations in every day language. It is used when an individual is experiencing a problem or challenge and is effective when used with rapport and respect for the individual's model of the world.

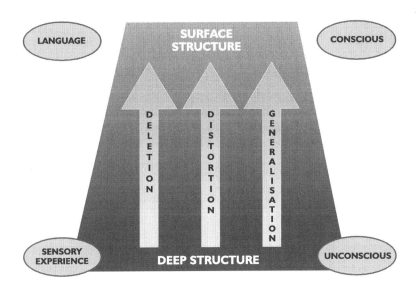

Distortion involves interpreting information in a way that changes it to fit the internal model of the world of the individual. Distortions can be empowering particularly when they involve creative elements. Many composers, artists, writers and poets distort their experience to create art. Distortions can also be disempowering particularly when we begin to attribute meaning to events that is based on fantasy, e.g. our boss looking at us in a particular way meaning that we are about to lose our job; or the distortions that can occur in psychological disturbance such as episodes of mania where an individual believes they have more money, resources, skills than evident in reality.

Deletions occur when we leave out portions of our experience. Korzybski (1948) considered that this was caused by individuals failing to recognise the intention, goal or meaning of the information that they receive from another person. We delete to help us reduce the amount of information that we need to process and to help us make sense of our feelings. It is easier to say *'I am unhappy'* than it is to explain precisely what we are unhappy about. Deletions often become the bug bears of organisations with problems being attributed to a process that has taken on a life of its own – *'there is no communication in this organisation'*. It is unclear what is not being communicated and to whom and entire departments are set up to develop communication strategies.

Generalisations form the basis of our learning. We group experiences together to avoid learning things over again. Generalisations can be helpful in summing up positive experiences – *'I am always successful'* which enables us to walk into the next experience believing and behaving as if we are going to be successful, leading to a greater likelihood that we will be. Occasionally we use generalisations to limit ourselves or to berate ourselves for not doing something – *'I have to achieve this'* or *'I can't be in a good relationship'*.

Process of the meta model

Individuals will offer linguistic clues to how they are currently distorting, deleting and generalising their experience.

Distortions

- **Mind Reads** – where the individual claims to know something about someone else, usually involving their state e.g. *'You don't like me'*

- **Lost Performative** – Where a judgement based on value is made, and the person who is making the judgement is not present in the sentence structure e.g. *'It's wrong to leave work before 5pm'*

- **Cause – Effect** – Where the cause is placed outside of the person and is attributed to someone or something else e.g. *'You make me so frustrated'*

- **Complex Equivalence** – Where 2 experiences are interpreted as being the same or equal to each other e.g. *'She looks at me in a funny way, (therefore) she doesn't like me'*

- **Presuppositions** – Where the person assumes certain things as true e.g. *If my boss cared, he would take the time to understand me'*. This assumes that the boss does not care, and that he does not understand the person.

Deletions

- ❧ Nominalisations – These are words that are processes that have been frozen and turned into a noun e.g. *'There is no communication in this organisation'*

- ❧ Unspecified Verbs – Where the verb is not applied to behavioural evidence e.g. *'He ignored me'*

- ❧ Simple Deletions – Where aspects of the sentence are missed out e.g. *'I am uncomfortable'*. We are not clear whether it is the chair, clothes or feelings that are uncomfortable

- ❧ Lack of Referential Index – The person or object in the sentence is missed out e.g. *'They don't like me'*

- ❧ Comparative Deletions – An action is being compared to something or somebody without specifying how the comparison is being made e.g. *'She is better than me'*.

Generalisations

- ❧ Universal Quantifiers – Where many experiences are grouped together as one, 'all', 'everyone', 'never', 'no-one', e.g. *'She always goes off sick'*

- ❧ Modal Operators of Necessity – Where the driver is an absolute and based on necessity and will include words like 'should', 'mustn't', 'got to', 'have to', e.g. *'I have to look after her'*

- ❧ Modal Operators of Possibility – Where the driver is optional and based on possibility and will include words like 'can', 'might', 'possible', e.g. *'I might turn up on time'*.

Procedure for using the meta model

There are some structured questions that enable you to assist individuals change their distortions, deletions and generalisations. There are some fundamental principles that assist the Meta Model to be used effectively. These include rapport with the individual; that the problem state is active for the person i.e. they are experiencing the problem now; you are congruent, respectful and believable in offering your question to them.

Pattern	Response

DISTORTIONS

I. Mind Reading:
Claiming to know someone's internal state. *E.g. "You don't like me"*

"How do you know I don't like you?"

2. Lost Performative:
Value judgements where the person doing the judging is left out. *E.g. "It's wrong to leave work before 5pm"*

"Who says it's wrong?"
"According to whom?"
"How do you know its wrong"

3. Cause – Effect:
Where cause is wrongly put outside the self. *E.g. "You make me so frustrated"*

"How does what I'm doing cause you to choose to feel frustrated?"

4. Complex Equivalence:
Where two experiences are interpreted as being synonymous: *E.g. "She looks at me in a funny way, she doesn't like me"*

"How does her looking at you in that way mean that she doesn't like you"
Or
"Have you ever looked at someone in a funny way that you liked?"

5. Presuppositions:
E.g. "If my boss cared, he would take the time to understand me"
There are 2 presuppositions in this sentence: a) the boss doesn't care b) the boss doesn't understand her

a) *"How do you know he doesn't care?"*

b) *"How do you know he doesn't understand you"*

DELETIONS

6. Nominalisations:
Process words that have been frozen in time, making them nouns. *E.g. "There is no communication in this organisation"*

"Who's not communicating what to whom?"
"How would you like to communicate?"

7. Unspecified Verbs:
E.g. "He ignored me"

"How, specifically?"

8. a) Simple Deletions:
E.g. "I'm very uncomfortable"

a) *"About what / whom?"*

b) Lack of Referential Index:
Fails to specify a person or thing.
E.g. "They don't like me"

b) *"Who, specifically, doesn't like you?"*

c) Comparative Deletions:
As in good, better, best, worst, more, less, most, least. *E.g. "She is better than me"*

c) *"Better at what?"* or *"Compared to what?"*

GENERALISATIONS

9. Universal Quantifiers:
Universal Generalisations like all, every, never, everyone, no one, etc.
E.g. "She always goes off sick"

Find counter examples. "Always?" "Has there ever been a time when she wasn't off sick?"

10. Modal Operators:
a) Modal Operators of Necessity:
should, shouldn't, must, must not, have to, need to, it is necessary.
E.g. "I have to look after her"

a) "What would happen if you did?" (What would happen if you didn't?").

b) Modal Operators of Possibility:
(or impossibility) can / can't, will / won't, may / may not, possible / impossible.
E.g. "I might turn up on time"

Also, "Or?"

b) "What would happen if you did?" or "What would happen if you didn't?"

Exercise

Record a television interview with a politician to watch. Notice the Meta Model linguistic patterns that they use and consider what alternative questions you might ask to discover their distortions, generalisations and deletions. Think about the impact that your questioning might have had compared to the interviewer. Are there any Meta Model responses or questions that the interviewer uses to elicit more information from the politician?

Applications

Problem solving – Use the Meta Model to rapidly get to the root cause of a problem. The Meta Model can be dovetailed with other problem solving technologies too.

Education – This model can be used when a student is struggling to understand a particular concept. The process enables the teacher to identify which part of the process might be causing difficulties for the student .

Coaching – The model provides an excellent coaching tool to enable the coach to develop insight into the coachee's model of the world. It can also be used to assist the coachee take responsibility for their actions, thoughts and behaviour, and provide impetus for change.

Therapy – To assist a client to see where they are attributing responsibility to someone or something else for their presenting problems.

Milton model

The Milton model emerged from Bandler and Grinder's modelling of the language patterns of Milton Erickson and was published in their work *'The Patterns of the Hypnotic Techniques of Milton H. Erickson, I & II.'* The Milton Model pattern is opposite to the Meta Model in that it involves abstract rather than specific language patterns.

Rationale

The conscious mind processes analytical and logical information that is predominantly detailed in structure. The unconscious mind processes information that is abstract, symbolic and metaphor in structure. Behaviours are driven by our unconscious mind therefore any communication that facilitates direct communication to the unconscious is more likely to influence change than the more conscious dialogue.

Evidence base

Curreen (1995) has utilised Milton Model language patterns with clients in a criminal justice setting. Using a case study approach he was able to demonstrate that the hypnotic language patterns of NLP were effective in facilitating the clients towards successful outcomes.

In the wider applications of Ericksonian work, Simpkins and Simpkins (2008) conducted an exploratory outcome comparison between Ericksonian approaches to therapy and brief dynamic therapy. The study used comparative pre and post tests using standardised assessment tools. No statistical differences were found, except on the symptoms check list, where Ericksonian therapy was found to be more effective.

Principles of Milton model

Erickson had a very effective style with clients and was able to rapidly set up unconscious communication and evidential change. There are a number of principles found within Erickson's work that underpin the structure of the Milton model.

- ෨ Communication is both verbal and non-verbal. Elements such as pauses, non verbal cues and voice inflection heighten the impact of the Milton model.

- ෨ There is acceptance of the client's model of the world and that their behaviour has a positive intention

- Clients have all the resources and natural abilities to overcome problems. The model works by helping clients to access these abilities.

- Language of the model is permissive rather than authoritarian so that people are given more choices with possibilities highlighted

- Ambiguous and vague language bypasses the client's conscious mind. The vagueness of the language means that the client then has to seek meaning from his or her own experience.

Process of the Milton model

The model consists of 22 different patterns. Each of the patterns consists of a linguistic structure that is adapted to the client's presenting situation and preferred outcome. Some of the patterns are the same as the Meta Model and are used to create distortions, deletions and generalisations.

- Mind Read - where you claim to know the thoughts or feelings of another without specifying the process by which you came to know the information

- Lost Performative - Value judgements where the person making the value judgement is left out of the sentence

- Cause & Effect - Where it is implied that one thing causes another. Implied Causatives include: 'makes', 'If . . . then . . .', 'As you . . . then you . . .'.

- Complex Equivalence - Where two things are equated; their meanings become equivalent

- Presupposition - The linguistic equivalent of assumptions

- Universal Quantifier - A set of words having universal generalisations or no referential index

- Modal Operator - Words which imply possibility or necessity and which form our 'rules' in life such as will, can, may, must, should, need

- Nominalisation - Process words (verbs) which have been frozen in time by making them into nouns that delete a great deal of information

- Unspecified Verb - The listener is forced to supply the meaning of the sentence

- Tag Question - A question added after a statement designed to displace resistance

- ❧ Simple deletions - Recovering awareness of experiences or sensory input
- ❧ Lack of Referential Index - Phrase in which the subject of the sentence is unspecified
- ❧ Comparative Deletion - Where the comparison is made and it is not specified as to what or to whom it was made
- ❧ Pace Current Experience - Where client's experience is described in a way which is undeniable
- ❧ Embedded commands and embedded questions - Directives that are embedded within the sentence which direct a person to do something. This is a double message and sends one message to the conscious mind and another message to the unconscious mind. Embedded questions are a sentence with a question included to which an overt response is not expected.
- ❧ Double Bind - A paradox which on the surface creates choice for the client but where either choice is acceptable
- ❧ Conversational Postulate - The communication has the form of a question to which the response is either a yes or a no
- ❧ Extended Quote - Distracting the conscious mind by the use of many referential indices
- ❧ Selectional Restriction Violation - A sentence that is not well formed in that an action is applied to an inanimate object
- ❧ Ambiguity – Phonological where a word is used that sounds the same but is spelt differently and so will have a different meaning; Syntactic where the function of a word cannot be immediately determined from the immediate context; Scope where it cannot be determined by linguistic context how much is applied to that sentence by some other portion of the sentence; Punctuation where pauses are added to a sentence to change the meaning
- ❧ Analogue Marking - Marking out a portion of the sentence verbally or non-verbally (with gestures)
- ❧ Utilisation - Utilise all that happens or is said using the client's language.

Procedure

In most instances only some of the Milton model patterns are used and usually in random order. I have given two examples here of sentence structures for each pattern and then placed them within a sentence for both scenarios.

Pattern	Coaching client who wants to develop confidence	Business audience who are focussed on maximising growth potential
Mind Read Claiming to know the thoughts or feelings of another without specifying the process by which you came to know the information	I know that you are wondering…	*I know that you are curious….*
Lost Performative Value judgements where the performer of the value judgement is left out	It's right to wonder about being confident	*It's good to focus on growth potential*
Cause & Effect Where it is implied that one thing causes another. Implied Causatives include: *C>E makes* *If . . . then . . .* *As you . . . then you . . .*	Because you have approached me for coaching, you have already taken the first step in becoming confident	*As we consider the small successes of last year, then we can place all of our attention on the growth potential of the business*
COMPLEX EQUIVALENCE Where two things are equated; their meanings become equivalent	Your work in coaching means that your confidence is growing	*Having growth potential means greater success for the business*
PRESUPPOSITION The linguistic equivalent of assumptions. Most everything presupposes something else	Have you recognised your growth in confidence?	*Your potential is already being released*
UNIVERSAL QUANTIFIER A set of words having universal generalisations or no referential index	Everyone knows it to be true	*Never has a company been in this place before*

Pattern	Coaching client who wants to develop confidence	Business audience who are focussed on maximising growth potential
MODAL OPERATOR Words which imply possibility or necessity, and which form our rules in life such as will, can, may, must, should, need	You must be aware of your own confidence levels growing	*You could begin to maximise your potential now*
NOMINALISATION Process words (verbs) which have been frozen in time by making them into nouns that delete a great deal of information	You have developed understanding	*Making that commitment to communication*
UNSPECIFIED VERB The listener is forced to supply the meaning of the sentence	And you can make sense...	*I want you to....*
TAG QUESTION A question added after a statement designed to displace resistance	Didn't you?	*Weren't we?*
SIMPLE DELETIONS Recovering awareness of experiences or sensory input	You might wonder....	*You have felt this...*
LACK OF REFERENTIAL INDEX Phrase in which the subject of the sentence is unspecified	Only you can develop this confidence	*One can begin to see the benefits of this opportunity*
COMPARATIVE DELETION Where the comparison is made and it is not specified as to what or to whom it was made	So this is happening more and more	*Sooner or later it will happen*

PACE CURRENT EXPERIENCE Where client's experience is described in a way which is undeniable	You have been seeing me to discuss this, you have already identified three things that you are going to take action on, and even as you think about arranging your next session, you will feel the confidence grow	*Being in this room, reviewing the figures, discussing opportunities that exist*
EMBEDDED COMMANDS Directives that are embedded within the sentence which direct a person to do something. This is a double message and sends one message to the conscious mind and another message to the unconscious mind	You will see this confidence grow	*You may find that the potential is created now or perhaps next month*
EMBEDDED QUESTIONS A sentence with a question included to which an overt response is not expected	I wonder which manager will notice your confidence increase first?	*Where will you see the biggest growth occur?*
DOUBLE BIND A paradox which on the surface creates choice for the client but where either choice is acceptable	You can experience the confidence now or as you drive home tonight	*Have you already recognised the potential that exists or will you see this after you have discussed those growth opportunities*
CONVERSATIONAL POSTULATE The communication has the form of a question, a question to which the response is either a yes or a no. If I want you to do something, what else must be present so that you will do it, and out of your awareness? It allows you to choose to respond or not and avoids authoritarianism	Do you think this is possible?	*Are you aware of the potential that this event creates?*

Pattern	Coaching client who wants to develop confidence	Business audience who are focussed on maximising growth potential
EXTENDED QUOTE Distracting the conscious mind by the use of many referential indices	Last month I was talking to a colleague and she reminded me about a seminar that she attended where the speaker discussed how effectively people access their own confidence	*I was in this other organisation that told me of a Canadian company that had focussed on similar possibilities and they reminded me of ....*
SELECTIONAL RESTRICTION VIOLATION A sentence that is not well formed in that an action is applied to an inanimate object	This room has been witness to your personal growth	*The walls of this building are champing at the bit for expansion*
AMBIGUITY **Phonological**	Hear/here your confident	*Too many people growth is already a possibility*
Syntactic Where the function (syntax) of a word cannot be immediately determined from the immediate context	Surprising confidence is what it is about	*They are growing potential within this business*
Scope Where it cannot be determined by linguistic context how much is applied to that sentence by some other portion of the sentence	Your deep insight and confidence	*Excellence your growth and potential*
Punctuation	You can already see.... confidence is present	*I want you to consider growing... potential is something that is attainable*

ANALOGUE MARKING Marking out a portion of the sentence verbally or non-verbally (with gestures)	As you recognise.... confidence is already present	You can appreciate... now... that potential is just around the corner
UTILISATION Utilise all that happens or is said, using the client's language	That's right, your coughing is evidence that you have already begun to change	Notice how the sun knows just when to shine on our potential

Coaching client who wants to develop confidence

'I know that you are wondering...and its right to wonder about being confident. Because you have approached me for coaching, you have already taken the first step in becoming confident. Everyone knows it to be true and you can make sense....that you will see this confidence grow.

Last month I was talking to a colleague and she reminded me about a seminar that she attended where the speaker discussed how effectively people access their own confidence and she said to me, your work in coaching means that your confidence is growing. Have you recognised your growth in confidence?'

Business audience who are focussed on maximising growth potential

'I know that you are curious.....that it's good to focus on growth potential. As we consider the small successes of last year, then we can place all of our attention on the growth potential of the business because having growth potential means greater success for the business. Never has a company been in this place before so you could begin to maximise your potential now. One can begin to see the benefits of this opportunity because sooner or later it will happen. Being in this room, reviewing the figures, discussing opportunities that exist, you may find that the potential is created now or next month.'

Exercise

Return to the recording of the interview with a politician. Listen to the interview again and notice how many Milton model patterns he/she was using. **What impact did these patterns have on you?**

Applications

Advertising – many successful adverts use hypnotic language patterns to encourage us to buy a product. Used ecologically and with a win: win in mind it is possible to utilise Milton model to facilitate a greater unconscious relationship to your product.

Coaching – To facilitate outcomes and access greater levels of resources that are held unconsciously.

Education – To unconsciously embed learning to enable rapid recall during examinations. To build confidence and self esteem in others.

Leadership – To utilise positive suggestions with yourself and others to maximise leadership potential.

Presentations – To embed the outcomes for the presentation and utilise accelerated learning techniques during training.

Linguistic presuppositions

Presuppositions are linguistic assumptions that we make. Everything we say includes some presuppositions. These assumptions act as a filter for what we distort, generalise and delete. For example, if someone makes the assumption *"I can't do ......"*, they will have deleted the possibility that they could do it and left themselves with far fewer choices. Paying attention to the presuppositions someone uses will allow you to help them explore where they are limiting themselves and to find out the strategies that they are using to achieve their current results.

Rationale

You can use presuppositions to help someone change their internal representation of an experience so that they have more choices and make the changes they want more quickly. They are particularly useful when setting up expectations of change. You can use presuppositions to create internal representations in yourself and others that can help bypass the resistance of the conscious mind. By being aware of the presuppositions you use in your internal dialogue you can help yourself to change your own internal representations. By being aware of the presuppositions others use you can help them change their internal representations.

Evidence base

Banner (2008), in conjunction with myself as Consultant, conducted a piece of research using linguistic presuppositions within letters accompanying employee satisfaction questionnaires to identify the effect that this had on return rate. Findings suggest that where linguistic presuppositions are used it is possible to increase the response rate. A second action based research by myself was conducted incorporating linguistic presuppositions within the quality standards of a tender submission to a Local Authority (Banner 2008). 60% of the evaluation of the submission was based on the quality standards. The organisation scored a total of 96.2% of the total possible score for this section demonstrating that the submission had to be specifically related to the Council's programme. The contract was awarded with a total value of £25 million.

Principles of linguistic presuppositions

People will assume certain things in the linguistic representation of their experience. These assumptions or presuppositions will provide an indication of their internal representation and will also have a direct influence on their experience.

Compare the impact of the following two sentences on someone's internal representation and their expectation of the experience:

'Trying to learn to ride a bicycle is a long and painful process'

'You will be surprised how quickly you can get your balance as you ride the bicycle'

Which sentence would have the greater chance of helping the person to achieve their outcome? Which would give them a useful internal representation for them to start out on their learning to ride a bicycle?

Presupposed in the first sentence are 3 assumptions.

Try - presupposes that they may not succeed

Long - it will take some time

Painful - it will be an unpleasant experience.

Presupposed in the second sentence are 4 assumptions.

Be surprised – presupposes that it happens spontaneously

Quickly – it will be a short process

Can get your balance – that balance is possible and they will achieve this

You ride the bicycle – presupposes that they can.

We can use presuppositions to facilitate others to have a more effective and outcome focussed internal representation.

Process of identifying linguistic presuppositions

There are 9 forms of linguistic presuppositions:

- ✵ Existence - Whether positive or negative the effect of the presupposition is still the same. This is usually a noun, a person, place or thing in a person's language based on their memories, decisions or values

- ✵ Modal Operators – The energy we use to organise our life

    Possibility - Whether or not the client believes something is possible. Cue words like *can, could, will, would, possible*

    Necessity - Cue words like *should, must, got to, have to,* that suggest the client is motivated by necessity

- ✵ Cause - Effect - Something that causes a specific effect; an implied connection. Cue words like *because, in order to, makes, as you . . . then you . . . , if . . . then"*

- ✵ Complex Equivalence - Occurs when you attach meaning to something specific. Cue words like derivatives of the verb to be, means, like that ascribe meaning to something

- ✵ Awareness - Verbs that imply perception of some sort. Cue words such as know, *realise, aware of,* and any of the senses

- ✵ Time - Verbs and verb tenses that move the client through time, *-ing* implies ongoing; *-ed* implies in the past. Cue words like *stop, now, yet, before*

- ✵ Adverb/Adjective - Verb/Noun (Modifiers) Where the modification is accepted as a presupposition

- ✵ Inclusive / Exclusive OR (the basis of Double Binds)

- ✵ Ordinal - Signifies numeric order or a list, and can use a word like *Firstly, Secondly, Lastly.*

Procedure

There are 2 steps to working with presuppositions. The first step is to identify what is presupposed in someone's language. The second step is to utilise the presuppositions to change them using a technique such as the Meta Model, or, to enable greater choice in the client through the use of Milton model.

I have given examples of presuppositions in a series of sentences, and then suggested some presuppositions for the clients who wanted to develop confidence and who wanted to maximise growth potential. The key to utilising presuppositions is to place them within a sentence so that the individual has to accept the presuppositions to make sense of the sentence.

The table below provides examples of how presuppositions are used in sentences.

Presupposition	Sentence
Existence Whether positive or negative, the effect of the presupposition is still the same. This is usually a noun, a person, place or thing in a person's language based on their memories, decisions or values	**Jane** knew that there was a **meeting** occurring
Modal Operators The energy we use to organise our life. **Possibility** - Whether or not the client believes something is possible. Cue words like *can, could, will, would, possible* which are known as Modal Operators	Jane saw that she **could** contribute in the meeting
Necessity - Cue words like should, must, got to, have to that suggest the client is motivated by necessity	Jane **had to** get her point across
Cause – Effect Something that causes a specific effect; an implied connection. Cue words like because, in order to, makes, as you . . . then you . . . , if . . . then"	As Jane went into the meeting this **made** her feel self conscious
Complex Equivalence Occurs when you attach meaning to something specific. Cue words like derivatives of the verb **to be, means, like** that ascribe meaning to something	Her manager looking at Jane **meant** that she became self conscious
Awareness Verbs that imply perception of some sort. Cue words such as *know, realise, aware of,* and any of the senses	Jane could **see** everyone **looking** at her

Presupposition	Sentence
Time Verbs and verb tenses that move the client through time, *-ing* implies ongoing; *-ed* implies in the past. Cue words *like, stop, now, yet, before*	Jane **decided** that it was time to leave the meeting **now**
Adverb/Adjective - Verb/Noun (Modifiers) Where the modification is accepted as a presupposition	Jane considered how **easily** she had made herself feel uncomfortable
Inclusive / Exclusive OR (the basis of Double Binds)	Jane hadn't decided whether to walk out straight away **or** after her presentation (inclusive) Jane hadn't decided whether to walk out **or** stay (exclusive)
Ordinal Signifies numeric order or a list, and can use a word like **Firstly, Secondly, Lastly**	The **last** thing Jane wanted to do was lose her boss's confidence

The table below gives examples of how presuppositions can be used with two different clients. The first client wants to develop confidence and the second client wants to maximise growth potential.

Presupposition	Client wanting to develop confidence	Business wanting to maximise growth potential
Existence Whether positive or negative, the effect of the presupposition is still the same. This is usually a noun, a person, place or thing in a person's language based on their memories, decisions or values	**You** already have **confidence**, it is just a question of accessing it	The **business** is clearly committed to **growth potential**

Modal Operators

The energy we use or organise our life

Possibility - Whether or not the client believes something is possible. Cue words like *can, could, will, would, possible* which are known as Modal Operators

It is **possible** for you to be even more confident

You **will** see a rapid change in your growth potential

Necessity - Cue words like *should, must, got to, have to* that suggest the client is motivated by necessity

You **have** to accept just how confident you are becoming

The business **must** harness it's growth potential

Cause – Effect

Something that causes a specific effect; an implied connection. Cue words like because, in order to, makes, as you . . . then you . . . , if . . . then"

As you feel more confident, **then** you will get feedback from others on the changes you have made

Wanting to develop growth potential **makes** the business even more likely to succeed

Complex Equivalence

Occurs when you attach meaning to something specific. Cue words like derivatives of the verb **to be, means, like that** ascribe meaning to something

Being confident **means** that you can achieve great things

To be committed to business growth **means** that more opportunities will arise

Awareness

Verbs that imply perception of some sort. Cue words such as *know, realise, aware of,* and any of the senses

Knowing yourself as you do, it is only a matter of time before you become **aware of** your increasing levels of confidence

Did you **realise** that the company has already identified that it can grow?

Presupposition	Client wanting to develop confidence	Business wanting to maximise growth potential
Time Verbs and verb tenses that move the client through time, *-ing* implies ongoing; *-ed* implies in the past. Cue words like, *stop, now, yet, before*	**Stop** thinking that confidence is out of reach	**Growing** your potential is one of the key areas for the business to focus on
Adverb/Adjective - Verb/Noun (Modifiers) Where the modification is accepted as a presupposition	How **effectively** would you like to see your confidence being applied in the workplace	We can **easily** access our growth potential
Inclusive / Exclusive OR (the basis of Double Binds)	You could be confident now **or** after we have agreed the next session date (inclusive) You increase your confidence this week **or** next week (exclusive)	Our growth potential can be identified through financial savings **or** increased productivity (inclusive) Will we see growth potential in this quarter **or** next quarter (exclusive)
Ordinal Signifies numeric order or a list, and can use a word like **Firstly, Secondly, Lastly**	Is it possible for you to **first** be aware of other peoples confidence in you?	**First** we will consider potential savings

Exercise

Listed here are some sentences that have presuppositions within them.
Think about how you might use presuppositions to enable the individual
to have a more useful internal representation. An example is given for
the first one.

Statement -   *'I'm not sure if I should go to the pub today'*

Presuppositions -   Existence of *I* and **pub**. Modal operator of
                               necessity **should**, time **today**, inferred exclusive or

Response -   *'You could choose to use your time to socialise
                               in other ways'*

Presuppositions -   Existence of **you**. Modal operator of possibility
                               could choose, time **time**, inferred exclusive or
                               other way

   I have presupposed that the person wants to socialise and that there
   are other ways of doing it than going to the pub.

Statement -   *'My boss really thinks I should apply for promotion'*

Presuppositions -   _____

                               _____

Response -   _____

                               _____

Presuppositions -   _____

                               _____

Statement -   *'I need to exercise to lose weight'*

Presuppositions -   _____

                               _____

Response -   _____

                               _____

Presuppositions -   _____

                               _____

Cont'd over page

Statement -	*'Do you really think it is possible to improve our bottom line this year?'*
Presuppositions -	_____
	_____
Response -	_____
	_____
Presuppositions -	_____
	_____
Statement -	*'I am never appreciated'*
Presuppositions -	_____
	_____
Response -	_____
	_____
Presuppositions -	_____
	_____

Applications

Coaching – Identify the presuppositions that your client is using in their language to help you and them gain insight into any unuseful beliefs that may be affecting their performance.

HR – Include presuppositions in your questionnaires and feedback forms. I worked with one company where we conducted a trial of introductory letters for the employee opinion survey. Response rates where higher where we used presuppositions to assume prompt return of the questionnaires.

Leadership – To utilise presuppositions in annual reports, management briefings and strategic plans.

Advertising – Adverts are an ideal place to use presuppositions. We see them often as non verbal and visual representations - *If I use this particular aftershave every gorgeous female will fall at my feet.* Used congruently, presuppositions can have a very powerful impact in advertisements.

Hierarchy of ideas

All change takes place at an unconscious level and the more you can help reach the unconscious the more you can help someone bring about change. You can use language to help someone go into trance or to bring them out of it. When we use abstract language we create trance and direct access to unconscious resources and potential. This is seen with the use of the Milton model. When we use specific detailed language such as the Meta model we bring someone out of trance and into a detailed sensory based experience. We can therefore use language as a powerful medium to affect someone's state which, from the communication model explained earlier in the book, directly influences our behaviour. Influential communicators are able to use abstract and detailed language with flexibility and individuals who are also able to introduce lateral thinking develop even greater flexibility in working towards solutions.

Rationale

The hierarchy of ideas is a process of chunking that enables you to move between levels of abstraction. We store information in chunks according to our levels of understanding as we make sense of the information. If I understand something well, I may hold only 1 chunk that has lots of smaller portions of information within it, whereas if I don't understand something as well e.g. operating a new piece of equipment, I may hold in conscious awareness only 1 or 2 pieces of information in each chunk. It is our ability to hold and process information that determines how abstract or how detailed we are in our thinking. There is also thought to be a correlation between left and right brain processes. Right brain processing focuses on the abstract and left brain on the detail and cognitive specific.

Chunking is the term used to describe what you do when you move groups of information either up levels of abstraction or down to levels of specificity.

Evidence base

There is one study (Duch et al 2008) that supports the neuroscientific basis for chunking. The study demonstrates that the right hemisphere is responsible for non verbal clustering or collection of chunks of information. The study also shows that as the person gathers more representations only the most useful aspects are retained, leading to higher degrees of accuracy in comprehension.

Principles of chunking

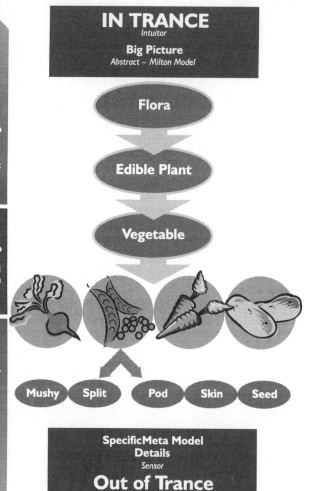

Chunking Up
Agreement

What is this an
example of?
For what purpose?
What is your intention?

In Mediation, chunk up
to get agreeement

Chunk up until you get
a nominalization

The Structure
of Intuition

Being able to chunk up
to find connections
and relationships, and
then chunk back down
and relate to the
current situation

It's rare to find a large
chunker that sorts for
information - they are
usually small chunkers.

What are examples
of this?
What specifically... ?

Any Meta Model
Question

Distinctions

Chunking Down

IN TRANCE
Intuitor

Big Picture
Abstract – Milton Model

Flora

Edible Plant

Vegetable

Mushy　Split　　Pod　Skin　Seed

SpecificMeta Model
Details
Sensor

Out of Trance

Process of chunking

Nominalization:
A noun that describes a non-tangible state. It is often a verb that has been changed into a noun, for example, happiness, motivation, achievement and success. Chunking up will often end in a nominalization.

Inductive:
(Chunking **up**)
Going from specific facts to a general conclusion.

Questions to ask:
What's the purpose of...?
What is this an example of...?
What's the intention of...?

This is useful when you are seeking agreement

Deductive:
(Chunking **down**)
Going from the abstract to specific details.

Questions to ask:
What specifically?
What are examples of these?

This is useful when you are seeking distinctions.

Lateral Thinking:

Coined by Edward DeBono to help people think more creatively. It involves chunking up to a higher level of abstraction, moving sideways on that level, finding other examples and then chunking down to find out how this relates to where you started.

Questions to ask:
What else would be an example of this?

Procedure

In negotiation, each party chunks up from the specifics to a higher level using the questions outlined above to examine the basic principles, fundamental needs and desires. By doing this they will most likely discover that there is some common aim or purpose that they all can agree with 'in principle.'

Examples of higher chunks:

To make sure that all parties are treated fairly

To make the world a better place

To increase profits for the business

To become more of who you really are.

Once the parties acknowledge that there is a shared aim, that they agree with the essence then it is possible to begin negotiation – with each party chunking down to plan the next steps. Often the role of the negotiator is to remind all parties that there is a fundamental point of agreement. There is a great deal that can be achieved by regularly returning to principles of agreement to validate that the negotiation is still on course and to remind people of their shared aims.

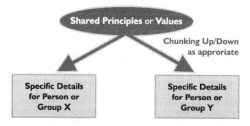

Exercise

Complete the following chart to notice how easily you can chunk and where some of your areas of development might be.

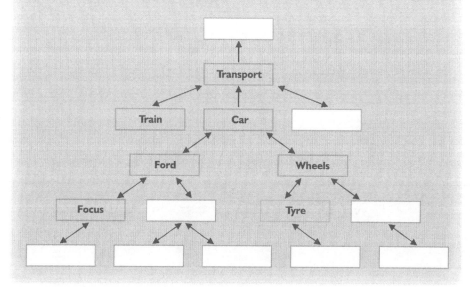

Applications

Learning– This model is excellent for developing mind maps to structure learning. By placing items of learning into categories it is possible to create a mind map such that an entire subject can be portrayed on one page.

Mediation – I have used this process many times in a mediation context to enable both parties to see the differing points of view and reach negotiated agreement.

Conflict resolution – This process enables each party to observe the motivations and goals of the person that they are in conflict with. By chunking up it is usually possible to reach a common agreement and then chunk back down to agree on the details.

Training – Effective trainers chunk their information using the hierarchy of ideas, taking information into finer levels of detail as the subject is understood by the group.

The way we communicate
with others and with ourselves
ultimately determines the
quality of our lives.

Anthony Robbins

Chapter Nine

Presenting Information

Getting the message over

INDIVIDUALS PREFER to receive information in their primary representational system. This then influences their state which in turn affects their physiology and drives their behaviour. Additional to this is a preference within information processing styles that can be useful when we think about how we structure information. Successful presenters are able to tailor their presentation such that it meets the information processing and learning needs of a diverse audience. This section will look at one of the structures of presenting information that is found within NLP – **4 Mat**.

 4 Mat

People learn differently and to assist them in learning easily we need to fit our presentations to their style of learning. The 4 mat system of learning and training styles has been adapted from the work of David Kolb (1971), a researcher from the University of Cleveland, who proposed that the major factors responsible for learning styles were based upon two poles:

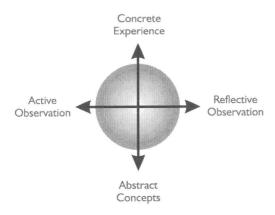

Bernice McCarthy (1987) was responsible for the synthesis of the results of various learning styles of the researchers in one cohesive model of learning. The result was the 4 Mat system which is one of the most widely used systems of learning and teaching in the world today.

The 4 Mat system explains learning styles in a way that is practical, easy to understand and easy to utilise in preparing presentations and trainings and as it is presented within NLP it is a synthesis of the work of Kolb and McCarthy.

Rationale

Kolb's studies into experiential learning are based in the theories of adult learning and development as they are portrayed by experts in psychology, constructivism, linguistics and human development: John Dewey, Kurt Lewin, Jean Piaget, William James, Carl Jung and Carl Rogers.

Kolb makes six assumptions about learning that help us to understand how people learn and develop through time. In summary these assumptions are:

- Learning is a process based on feedback and engagement rather than an outcome
- All learning is relearning with the aim of building on existing ideas and formulating new concepts from an existing base
- Learning is driven by conflict, difference and disagreement where we attempt to resolve these polarities. To resolve these we move through polarity opposites of reflection and action, and thinking and feeling.
- Learning involves integrating how we think and feel in the world to enable us to function as a whole person
- Learning is derived from our interactions with the world where we integrate new experiences into our existing model of the world
- Learning as a process creates knowledge and is constructed within our world rather than directly received from it.

McCarthy's understanding of Kolb's work developed into theories of left and right brain processing and the use of learning styles to develop fully integrated and whole brain functioning.

Left brain learners are logical, rational, and sequential in that things have to be in order for them to learn. They are serial and build on previous learning, and verbal with the opportunity to ask questions.

Right brain learners are intuitive, emotional, holistic and view things from many perspectives. They are parallel in their processing and can run multiple concepts at the same time. They can transfer learning rapidly into other contexts and alongside other concepts, and tactile with the opportunity to experience and feel their learning.

Evidence base

I can find no empirical evidence that has measured the effectiveness of the use of the 4 mat teaching and learning system as it is portrayed within NLP. There are studies that both support and question the internal validity and reliability of Kolb's learning styles inventory (Kayes 2005, Koob 2003).

Principles of 4 Mat

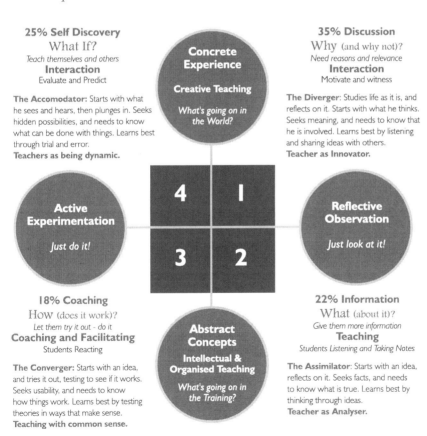

25% Self Discovery
What If?
Teach themselves and others
Interaction
Evaluate and Predict

The Accomodator: Starts with what he sees and hears, then plunges in. Seeks hidden possibilities, and needs to know what can be done with things. Learns best through trial and error.
Teachers as being dynamic.

35% Discussion
Why (and why not)?
Need reasons and relevance
Interaction
Motivate and witness

The Diverger: Studies life as it is, and reflects on it. Starts with what he thinks. Seeks meaning, and needs to know that he is involved. Learns best by listening and sharing ideas with others.
Teacher as Innovator.

Concrete Experience
Creative Teaching
What's going on in the World?

Active Experimentation
Just do it!

Reflective Observation
Just look at it!

4 **1**
3 **2**

18% Coaching
How (does it work)?
Let them try it out - do it
Coaching and Facilitating
Students Reacting

The Converger: Starts with an idea, and tries it out, testing to see if it works. Seeks usability, and needs to know how things work. Learns best by testing theories in ways that make sense.
Teaching with common sense.

22% Information
What (about it)?
Give them more information
Teaching
Students Listening and Taking Notes

The Assimilator: Starts with an idea, reflects on it. Seeks facts, and needs to know what is true. Learns best by thinking through ideas.
Teacher as Analyser.

Abstract Concepts
Intellectual & Organised Teaching
What's going on in the Training?

Process of 4 Mat

Why

'Why' thinkers are known as **Divergers**. They are primarily interested in personal meaning and in a learning situation they need to have their reason for learning fulfilled. They will integrate their learning experiences with their own sense of self.

'Why' learners:

- ಖ Enjoy meaning, clarity and integrity
- ಖ Become personally involved in examples and experiences
- ಖ Seek commitment from the educator and from themselves
- ಖ Exercise their authority on whether they participate or not
- ಖ Learn by listening and exchanging ideas
- ಖ Value insightful thinking
- ಖ Work towards harmony
- ಖ Assimilate reality
- ಖ Perceive information concretely and process it thoughtfully
- ಖ Are interested in people and culture
- ಖ Believe in their own experience and are good at looking at concrete situations from any perspective
- ಖ Most like to be like those that they respect.

Strengths of a 'Why' learner

- ಖ Innovative and imaginative
- ಖ Ideas people
- ಖ Operate through social integration and value clarity.

What

'What' learners are known as **Assimilators**. They are primarily interested in what they know and what you want them to know. They need facts to help them develop conceptual understanding.

'What' learners:

- ಖ Form theories and concepts
- ಖ Seek facts and continuity
- ಖ Need to know what the experts think
- ಖ Seek goal attainment and personal effectiveness

- Exercise authority with assertive persuasion
- As leaders, they are brave and protective
- Learn by thinking through ideas
- Value sequential thinking
- Need details
- Form reality
- Are more interested in ideas than people
- Perceive information abstractly and processes reflectively
- Critique information and collect data
- Are thorough and industrious
- Re-examine facts if situations are perplexing
- Enjoy traditional classrooms
- Function by thinking things through and adapting to experts.

Strengths of a 'What' learner

- Creating concepts and models

How

'How' learners are known as **Convergers**. They are primarily interested in finding out if what they know (about what others know) is valid. They need to know how things work.

'How' learners:

- Practise and personalise their learning
- Seek usability, utility, solvency and results from their learning
- Need to know how things work
- Exercise authority by reward and punishment
- Lead by inspiring quality
- Learn by testing theories in ways that seem most sensible
- Value strategic thinking, are skills oriented and re-organise reality
- Perceive information abstractly and process it actively
- Use factual data to build designed concepts
- Enjoy solving problem
- Resent being given answers
- Need hands-on activities
- Restrict judgement to concrete things

- Have limited tolerance for fuzzy ideas

- Need to know how what they do will help them in life

- Function largely through inferences drawn from their bodies, their kinaesthetic selves.

Strengths of a 'How' learner

- Practical application of ideas.

What If

'What if' learners are known as **Accommodators**. They are primarily interested in finding out if what they know can create new possibilities. They need to know what would happen if…?

'What If' learners:

- Integrate experiences and application

- Seek hidden possibilities and excitement

- Need to know what can be done with things

- Exercise authority through common vision

- Lead by energising people

- Learn by trial and error and self-discovery

- Seek influence

- Enrich reality

- Perceive information concretely and process it actively

- Are adaptable to change and even relish it

- Like variety and excel in situations calling for flexibility

- Tend to take risks

- Sometimes seen as pushy

- Are at ease with people

- Often reaches accurate conclusions in the absence of logical justification

- Function by acting and testing experience.

Strengths of a 'What If' learner

 • Action oriented

 • Carry out plans

Procedure

In presenting information it is important to include some principle elements in each quadrant. As you structure your presentation include the following elements for each section and deliver the presentation in the sequence of Why, What, How, What If.

Under each section I have given examples of what I would include if I was doing a presentation on Rapport to an audience of Sales personnel.

Why

 • Goal or outcome for the presentation

 • Generate interest by making it directly relevant to the audience

 • Use examples that will motivate them.

Example to Sales people on Rapport

 • Would you like to increase your sales further?

 • What percentage of sales do you think are influenced by the relationship?

 • Would you be interested to know how excellent sales people get results?

 • Have you ever wondered where something went wrong in a sales meeting?

What

 • What are you going to tell them?

 • What else might they also know it as e.g. if you are going to talk about confidence as your presentation topic, you may also want to refer to self belief or self esteem

 • Tell them why it works, what might the rules be regarding the subject

 • What processes do they need to understand?

 • What does the technique involve?

Example to Sales people on rapport

- Overview definition of rapport – e.g. rapport is about setting up trust with your customers

- Rapport is also known as 'being in tune', 'connecting', 'tuning in', 'being on the same page'

- Discuss the 7/38/55 rule described in chapter 4

- Explain how rapport works

- Give an outline of the kinds of things to match in rapport

- Discuss the differences between matching and mirroring

- Demonstrate the process of body matching to them using another member of the group.

How

- Give clear instructions on the exercise

- Give feedback.

Example to sales people on rapport

- Work in pairs, person A and person B. Have a dialogue about something such as your holiday and person A, match B's body language and notice what happens. After 5 minutes, discuss what you have observed and then swap roles.

What If

- Seek feedback and learning

- Remind them of what they have learnt and observed

- Focus their learning to transfer it to the real world.

Example to sales people on rapport

- How did you get on, what have you learnt?

- How do you think you are going to use this back in the field?

- Are there any situations where you would not want to use it?

Exercise

Consider a presentation that you are planning to give or a report that you are due to write. Structure it in the 4 Mat below.

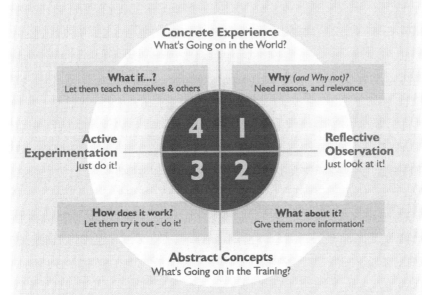

Applications

Interviews – Prior to the interview determine who is on the interview panel, the objectives of the organisation and your key result areas. Present information in the 4 Mat ensuring that you use the information that you have sourced to plan the presentation. In your What If section have some questions prepared that presuppose you have been appointed to the role.

Presentations – To structure your presentation and have just the 'big picture' of the 4 mat on a prompt card.

Education – To structure teaching sequences so that all learning styles are covered.

Advertising – When I first learnt this model I adapted all of our course information so that it commenced with Why someone might be interested in attending the programme. What key skills and topics would be learnt and covered. How the programme was run such as times, dates and venue, and What If they wanted to book such as prices and contact details.

Chapter Ten

Motivating and
Influencing Others

Inspiring others to succeed

AS WE have already seen from the Communication Model and subsequent chapters there are many different influences that affect our behaviour. We create internal representations through a process of filtering information. Two of the deep filters that influence how we process information are directly responsible for our motivation and attitudes. By understanding these filters we can develop insight into how we and other people are motivated, what drives us to do what we do and also how to utilise these filters to get the best out of ourselves and others. In this chapter I will review these two filters:

 Values and **Metaprogrammes**.

Values

Values are the principles that we live by and are how we apply worth to something. Values give us our motivation: if we really want something we are sufficiently motivated to go and get it. In the same way if we really don't want something we work very hard to avoid it occurring. Our values are deep unconscious filters and drive all of our behaviours. We use values as criteria by which we judge things and when our values are met or matched we feel a sense of satisfaction, harmony or rapport. When values are not met or matched we often feel dissatisfied, incongruent or violated.

Rationale

There are a number of theories that underpin values work in NLP: James' (1884) theory of human development; Maslow (1943) and his self actualisation theory; Graves (1965) and his theories on the environmental influence on our values and the subsequent work of Beck and Cowan (1996); and, Massey (1979) and his perspective on values and the developing personality.

In essence each of the above theorists proposes that we evolve and grow over time in response to environmental conditions. In effect, they propose that the things we regard as important are in large measure influenced by the context in which those things are challenged. Some of the main influences on our values are:

- ❧ Family – Especially up to the age of adolescence. At adolescence the individual transfers their primary sense of security to their peer group.

- ❧ Friends – The values of friends have a much greater impact during adolescence

- ❧ Church or Religion – Religious influences, teachings and traditions play a major role in formulating our values. These often become the rules by which the individual feels judged.

- ❧ School – The type of school, relationship between the school and the family, the subjects taught and relationships with teachers

- ❧ Geography/ Location – Where you grow up and the local society can have a major impact on values

- ❧ Economics – Within the family and the wider society

- ❧ Media – The direct messages that come into the home via television, radio, dvds, the internet, newspapers

- ❧ Major Historical Events – Can have an impact on how you think about yourself

- ❧ Significant Emotional Events – Specific events such as deaths, births, marital endings, moving house, major illness occur in our lives and can have a significant impact on our values.

In Massey's (1979) reflection on how the events in our lives shape our values he proposes different generational motivators based on the values that became imprinted as each generation was growing up:

- ❧ Traditionalists - Born before 1947. They liked to be in control of the system that they helped to build. As a reflection of the war era they tend to prefer to do things in groups and will look up to and trust authority figures. They tend to believe in order and will often dress more formally, preferring to be referred to by surnames when addressed by people they are not familiar with. They have a hard work ethic and prefer stability.

- ❧ Harmonisers. Also known as nuagers or boomers - Born 1947 – 1965 They have some drives similar to the next generation below them, however they received their value set from the Traditionalists. They enjoy hard work, competition and success. They prefer working through the team and tend to reject rules and regulations. They tend to speak directly and use body language to communicate. They reflect the freer thinking that emerged after the second world war and the growth in the humanist movement in the 1950's and early 1960s and are positive in their outlook on life. They tend to prefer opportunities for personal development and will read self-help books or attend workshops on personal development.

- ❧ Rejectionists – Also known as Generation X - Born 1966 – 1977. This was the start of modern-day technology so this generation tend to be entrepreneurial. They want to participate in decisions that affect them. They will work and play hard with short spans of attention. They tend to be informal in their dress and actions and work is just a small part of life. They are comfortable with change and look for instant solutions.

- ❧ Nxters or Generation Y - Born 1978 – 1995. They value autonomy and will usually feel quite secure in who they are. They tend to have a positive outlook on life and will address problems immediately as they come up.

Evidence base

Young (1995) has conducted a qualitative study reviewing the effects of NLP interventions including NLP based values work on a leadership population. Her study suggests that leaders made lasting progress that resulted in growth and change that was still evident one year later.

Campbell et al (2006) have identified that Rapport is essential for the exploratory phase of the customer relationship in sales and meeting values is one element of this.

Clark (2008) and Coalter (2008) have both used the NLP Values framework for proposing a conceptual framework for identifying leadership values and beliefs within the NHS.

Principles of values

Values provide the basis for our motivation and are directly linked to our beliefs, attitudes and behaviours.

Values are sometimes referred to as Criteria, the standards and evidence we apply in order to make decisions and judgements. Our criteria will define and shape the desired states that we seek and will determine the evidence we will use to evaluate our success with respect to these desired states. Our values are subjective: two individuals can have the same value and yet act quite differently in similar situations. This is because they have different forms of evidence for judging whether their criteria have been met or not. Within our values we will have a Hierarchy. As we evaluate our actions the more important values are usually checked first. After the more important values are found and satisfied then the less important values become important. Each of our values will have a series of Beliefs that support them. Beliefs are convictions that we hold to be true. They are statements about our internal representations and they are attached or related to a certain value, e.g. 'I value honesty and I believe it is important to tell the truth'. Our Attitudes are formed from the collection of beliefs and values around a certain subject e.g. I may have an attitude of demonstrating respect to others because I believe that all people deserve to be respected, and my value is Equality. Our Behaviour is a result of our attitudes.

The most commonly referenced work to support the theory of values in NLP is that of Massey (1979). Massey proposed that our development consists of generalised learning in response to positive and negative states. These responses become our basic motivational drives and lead to the creation of our core values, e.g. if we feel positive and happy when being part of a family unit as we grow up, this will become important to us as a value in adulthood. If we feel negative and unhappy when being part of a family and only feel happy when on our own and being independent, we may value independence more than the family. These developmental periods are also impacted by the significant emotional events that occur in our lives, e.g. if a parent loses a job and we experience a period of poverty, security may become a core value in later life.

Imprint Period – This is the development of our filters and continues up to the age of 6-7. We develop our basic programming at this time particularly the unconscious motivational drivers related to emotional states.

Modelling Period – This is the time when we consciously and unconsciously model basic behaviour from age 7 through to the start of adolescence. We model the principal adults in our life and we start to become more aware of the differences between ourselves and others. We notice the behaviour of friends and family and will often copy them. We begin to develop heroes and may also model their value set. Our major values about life tend to be laid down during this period.

Socialisation Period – Social interaction expands rapidly at the start of adolescence the age of which will vary according to each individual. We start to develop peer and intimate relationship values most of which will be used throughout the rest of our lives. Our core values tend to be set during this period and these do not change unless there is a significant emotional experience. Our more conscious values will and do change and evolve continually as we change and grow over time.

Our values apply in a range of different Contexts. We may have one value set for home, another for work and a different set for our health. Alignment in values occurs when each of the values in context support the other contexts and our overall life values. We may have a value of security in our career that is mirrored by security in our personal relationship and security in friendships. These values may change over time as well as across contexts e.g. security may be important while we are bringing up a family and become less important once any children have left home.

Process of working with values

Values provide meaning for the decisions that we make as well as driving our motivation. Within motivation we will either move 'towards' the things that we want or 'away from' the things that we don't want. This motivational drive is an internal regulatory process that is developed during infancy (Wake 2009 p77). Robbins (1991 p347 -357) discusses how our values act as our 'life compass' in *Awaken the Giant Within*, and Lazarus (2006 p78-82) considers how the motivational element of values affects success or failure in a sports context.

It is important to identify the context of the values the main values including the most important or core values, and the motivation direction. People who move towards the things that they want find it easier to achieve things and sustain their achievement than people who move away from things. Moving towards is a character trait seen within entrepreneurs and action oriented individuals. Individuals who move towards what they want will often use language such as: *'I want to xxx', I can xxx, I could xxx, it will give me xxxx, I will achieve xxxx.'* People who move away are usually very good at planning, procrastination and considering the consequences of potential actions. Moving away from is a character trait seen within individuals who are more risk averse or cautious in their actions and is an ideal attribute for working in health and safety and other caution based careers. Individuals who move away from what they don't want will often use language such as: *'I don't want yyy', I can't yyy', 'it would hurt/be uncomfortable/make me sad etc etc'*, or they may dissociate and refer to themselves in the third person: *'you would see yourself developing zzz', you might be successful'*.

Procedure

Values occur in different contexts and in coaching it is more effective to elicit values and work with them inside of a certain context.

The contexts of values

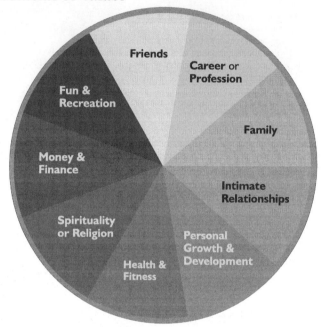

There are a number of steps to eliciting values:

☞ Identify what is important to someone about the context in which you are eliciting the values.

'What's important to you now about _____ ?'.
This question is continued until up to 8 values are identified.

☞ The next step is to identify why each value is important to the person. As values are unconscious it takes a few questions before the motivational drive becomes apparent. The following questions are asked to access the unconscious motivational drive: 'Why is *(Value #1)* important?'.
When the client gives you their answer, ask the next question inserting their answer: 'Why is *(answer)* important?'. When they give you the answer to this, ask the next question inserting their answer: 'Why is *(answer)* important?'. This is done for each of the individual values.

I have given examples of towards and away from motivations for the value Respect.

Towards motivation

e.g.	**'Why is Respect important to you?**
Answer	*'Because I want to value other people for their contribution'*
Question	'Why is <u>valuing other people for their contribution</u> important?'
Answer	*'Because I enjoy seeing people succeed'*
Question	'Why is <u>enjoying seeing people succeed</u> important?'
Answer	*'Because then I know that I have contributed my best'*

Away from motivation

e.g.	**'Why is <u>Respect</u> important to you?**
Answer (towards answer)	*'Because I hate it when people don't get respected '*
Question	'Why is <u>hating it when people don't get respected</u> important?'
Answer	*'Because I think it is wrong to not respect people'*
Question	'Why is <u>'it's wrong to not respect people'</u> important?'
Answer	*'Because life becomes so depressing if you don't get respect from other people'*

- ❧ The next step is to rank the values in order of importance. There are a couple of questions that can be used to help the ranking process. *'Now will you please number the values according to their relative importance to you',* or *'Of these values, which is the most important to you? Or 'if you could only have one of these values, which would it be'.* Then *'Assuming you have (value chosen), if you could have one more, which would it be?'* This continues until all of the values are ranked in order of importance.

- ❧ Reorder and rewrite the list of values according to their importance

- ❧ The client can then use this ranking and understanding of their motivation direction (i.e. 'towards' or 'away from') to select jobs, houses, relationships, health choices, hobbies etc.

There are a number of processes that are used with values in NLP and these are best learnt in a taught and supervised environment as they involve working with and changing the internal value and belief structure of a client to achieve greater success. These processes are taught at Master Practitioner level and require an understanding of other change processes within NLP.

Exercise

- List your values for a specific context using the process above. You may want to also list your motivation direction. Some people find it easier to have this done by someone else so that the answers are unconscious rather than consciously thought about.

- Rank your values in order of importance.

- Use the ranking to help you make a decision in the context that you elicited the values in. Decide the top 3 values and then work out on a scale of 1-10 how much each value would be met if you made the decision. I have given an example below.

Context – Career

Top values – Success, Financial Reward, Working with a great team

Ranking – 1 = low attainment of value,

10 = high attainment of value

Job	Success	Financial Reward	Working with a great team	Total
Promotion to manager at a supermarket	6	5	10	21
Change to apply for Manager at a clothing store	3	5	0	8
Career change to become a teacher	10	4	0	14

Applications

Coaching – Working with values is probably one of the most powerful processes that you can use as a coach. It can be used to assist with career choices, identify motivational blocks such as away from patterns that keep occurring or to develop insight for the coachee.

Change management– By understanding the values of an organisation you can assist greater alignment towards organisational values during a change management process.

Recruitment – Advertise and recruit against a specific value set. These values questions can also be asked at interview.

Mentoring – By helping you and the mentee understand their values in a number of different contexts will enable you to assist them in making life choices.

Couples counselling or mediation – By eliciting and gaining understanding of the values and motivational drives for individuals it is possible to discuss where compromise may be possible. We are usually more willing to compromise on our lower order values than the most important ones.

Metaprogrammes

In life some people seem very similar to ourselves and other people seem to be very different and we may even have difficulty understanding their approach to life. These differences in character are influenced by our **metaprogrammes**.

Metaprogrammes are content-free filters and change across different contexts.

Rationale

People have some characteristics in common and differ in other characteristics. One can either emphasise the similarities or the differences. At the extremes are 2 opposing viewpoints. At one extreme is the view that all people are basically the same, they are just at a different stage of their development i.e. all people are like us, thus to understand people we only need to understand ourselves. This leads to a projection of our values, beliefs and internal processes on others. At the other extreme is the view that all people are different. Each person is unique, has a different history and model of the world. Life may be either a process of discovering and appreciating these differences or of trying to reduce these differences and change other people to be as much like ourselves as possible.

Both of these two extremes are based on a kernel of insight and are flawed. The simple fact is that people have some characteristics in common and many in which they differ. Throughout modern psychology there have been various forms of reductionism in trying to understand and codify the different personality character types.

Summarised below are the main theories as they have been developed through time.

> ## Hippocrates **5 BC**

4 types of temperament for human mood and behaviour.

- Choleric/ phlegmatic/ melancholic/ sanguine

> ## Adickes **1907**

4 world views
- Dogmatic/ agnostic/ traditional/ innovative

> ## Adler **1920**

4 mistaken goals that people pursue when upset
- Recognition/ power/ service/ revenge

> ## Kretschmer **1925**

4 temperaments
- hyperesthetic *(too sensitive)*
- anaesthetic   *(too insensitive)*
- melancholic   *(too serious)*
- hypomanic   *(too excitable)*

> ## Springer **1928**

4 human values
- Religious/ theoretic/ economic/ artistic

> ## Jung **1920's**

8 types generated by 3 sets of polarities
- Extroverted Sensation
- Extroverted Intuition
- Extroverted Feeling
- Extroverted Thinking
- Introverted Sensation
- Introverted Intuition
- Introverted Feeling
- Introverted Thinking

- Isabel Myers and Kathleen Briggs **1950's**

  16 types generated by 4 polarities

  - **I** = Introverted   **E** = Extroverted
  - **S** = Sensation   **N** = Intuition
  - **T** = Thinking   **F** = Feeling
  - **P** = Perceiving   **J** = Judging

- Bandler, Cameron-Bandler, Gordon, Dilts, Meyers-Anderson **1980's**

  7 original metaprogrammes
  - Approach to problems
  - Time frame
  - Chunk size
  - Locus of control
  - Mode of comparison
  - Approach to problem solving
  - Thinking style

  16 complex metaprogrammes

  3 communication style

- Woodsmall and James **1988**

  Metaprogrammes and Values Inventory™

  MPVI™

- Bailey and Stewart **1990's**

  Biodata™   IVP Profile™

- Charvet **1990's**

  Lab Profile™

- Lowenthal **Late 1990's**

  Reality systems model with further distinctions of metaprogrammes

Evidence base

There are a multitude of studies that support and validate the Myers Briggs Type Inventory as a psychological assessment tool. I have been unable to source any empirical studies that specifically measure the use of the complex metaprogrammes.

Principles of metaprogrammes

Metaprogrammes are overarching or 'meta' patterns or 'programmes' of behaviour that we demonstrate in specific contexts. They change across contexts and also as we grow and develop. As we develop through time we form generalisations in our patterns of behaviour as useful learning responses: these become our metaprogrammes and they help us to build coherence and meaning from our experiences. Metaprogrammes can also act as deletion filters in that they help us to focus on specific aspects of our experience while deleting other aspects.

Metaprogrammes are explicit formations of patterns in thought and behaviour and they are most effectively used as a guide to understand behaviour rather than as a medium through which we can label people.

In the context of NLP, metaprogrammes are derived from Jung's (1921/1972) perspective on personality types and then further developed by Myers and Briggs (Myers 1962).

Jung's 8 types are divided into three sets of polarities: Introversion/Extroversion as a demonstration of external behaviour; Sensor/Intuitor as a demonstration of internal process or internal representation in NLP; Thinker/Feeler as a demonstration of internal state. Introverts will operate through Sensor, Intuitor, Thinker or Feeler. Extroverts will also operate across these responses. Within NLP these are further developed through Myers Briggs to include the Adaption Operator which is the Judger/Perceiver axis of adaptation response to events or how we perceive the world and adapt our response to it.

Simple metaprogrammes

    ℂ Introverts – tend to make up about 25% (Woodsmall) of the average population. Their behaviour is territorial and they have limited numbers of relationships. Where relationships exist, they are deep, intense and long lasting over many years. Introverts prefer to reflect, thinking before speaking. They also prefer to conserve their energy.

    ℂ Extroverts – make up about 75% of the population. Their behaviour is externally focussed and usually involves extensive multiple relationships. They enjoy expending their energy and will become fully involved in external events. They are gregarious and will usually speak before thinking.

    ℂ Sensors – make up about 70% of the population. Sensors base their reality on the here and now and realism. They prefer facts, down-to-earth and rational thinking. Practical ideas and working through things is essential to their understanding.

- **Intuitors** – make up about 30% of the general population. Intuitors base their reality on random concepts that are often developed through inspirational and fantasy thinking. They speak in general language and prefer a more ingenious approach to problem solving.

- **Thinkers** – Approximately half the population will have a thinking based state response to information and external events. Thinkers are very objective in their reactions and will prefer to see decisions made in a just, firm and clear manner. They enjoy thinking about policy and will critique events for the most rational view. They are good at dealing with situations that require a detached or dissociated perspective.

- **Feelers** – 50% of the population are more subjective in their decision making. They operate in response to circumstances and can be persuaded to take a more humane view that is based on social values. They appreciate harmony and enjoy being involved in the more interactive components of decision making.

- **Judger** – Judgers make up about 50% of the average population. Judgers can be identified by their structure and requirement for fixed deadlines They make excellent timekeepers and prefer to operate to schedules They have a high need for planning and closure and will sometimes consider that events are out of control if they can't be closed, planned or fixed.

- **Perceiver** – Perceivers make up about 50% of the average population. Perceivers have a much more flexible relationship with time, resulting in a 'wait and see' attitude. They tend to adapt to external circumstances and will go with the flow, often leaving plans open-ended. They are more open in their decision making and approach things either spontaneously or may be tentative if they are uncertain. Deadlines are a misnomer to perceivers.

Complex metaprogrammes

There are 16 complex metaprogrammes and an additional 3 communication preference metaprogrammes.

- **Direction Filter** - There are two reasons why anyone does anything. Towards people do things because they want to achieve certain outcomes or goals or attain certain things. They are good at priorities and may be oblivious to what's not working. Away from people do things because they want to avoid certain situations or things. They have trouble maintaining goal focus and are easily distracted by negative situations. There is a spectrum for towards and away from with some people being either totally or mainly towards, some being equally towards and away, and some being either mainly or totally away from.

ど Reason Filter - People will respond to procedures in one of two ways either options or procedures. Options people are good at developing new procedures and at figuring out alternatives to a procedure. They are very poor at following procedures and will feel almost compelled to improve or alter them. Procedures people are good at following procedures but they do not know how to generate them. They are good at doing a task 'the right way'. They have an almost compulsive need to complete a procedure.

ど Frame of reference - There are two fundamental ways of evaluating any person, situation, experience or thing. Internal people evaluate things on the basis of what they think is appropriate. They provide their own motivation and make their own decisions. They have difficulties accepting other people's direction and feedback. They may gather information from others but they decide about it. External people evaluate things on the basis on what other people think is appropriate. They need other people to provide guidance, motivation and direction. Some people will have a balanced internal and external check.

ど Convincer Representational Filter - People make decisions through the four senses. They do things because they either look right (see), sound right (hear), feel right (feel) or make sense (ad – auditory digital).

ど Convincer Demonstration Filter - People will make decisions according to the number of times or length of time that they experience something. They will have one of four responses: Automatic, where they don't need convincing they just are; Number of times, where they need to experience something a set number of times before they are convinced; Period of time, where they will need a period of time to lapse before they are convinced; or, Consistent, where it doesn't matter what you do they will never be convinced.

ど Management Direction Filter – This metaprogramme identifies someone's preference in a management situation and gives a good indication of whether someone will be able to manage effectively or not. Individuals will either respond as Self and others, where they have good management attitudes to themselves and other people; Self only, where they can manage their own workload and prefer not to manage others; Others only, where they are very good at directing other people and can't direct themselves, so will need clear tasks and job role to follow; and, Self but not others, where they are good at directing themselves, can direct others but prefer not to.

- Action Filter - Action level sort is proactive, reactive or both. This has to do with the toward and away from sort. It has to do with intensity of movement with respect to that sort and is how fast they are going to move. People will be proactive where they will just get on with it and need no prompting; reactive, where they let things take their course; both, where they will have the energy to pursue goals and will also take the time to check the consequences of their actions; and, inactive, where they don't like to do anything.

- Work Style or Affiliation Filter – determines how well people will work together in a group. Independent player works best when alone and in control; Team player gets their rewards from working in a team; Management player can take responsibility and doesn't have to be in charge.

- Work Preference Filter or Organisational Sort – This is whether we prefer activity or people. When asking a person about a work situation that they enjoyed most you will hear in their language their preference for what they have become involved in: people, things or the system.

- Primary Interest Filter - This has to do with what people are primarily interested in, in life. Individuals will have a preference for people, place, things, activity or information.

- Chunk Size Filter - Chunk size is specific (sensor) or global (intuitor). Chunking can be considered equivalent to going from the big picture to the details (Global to Specific) and the details of the big picture (Specific to Global).

- Relationship Filter - If you ask someone what the relationship between objects is you will get radically different views of the world. Some people will respond with Sameness, some will respond with Sameness with exception, where they are aware of similarities first and then notice exceptions to this, Sameness and Differences equally, Differences with Exception, where they notice the differences and then become aware of some exceptions to this, and Differences.

- Emotional Stress Response - The purpose of the stress response is to determine how a person will respond under stress. This will depend on whether a person is thinking or feeling or they may access feeling first and then move to thinking – choice.

- Time Storage Filter - There are two views of time. In time and through time. In time people, usually, but not always, have their time lines arranged front to back and are usually 'perceivers' in that they have less awareness of time. Through time people usually, but not always, have their time lines arranged side to side or in a V in front of them and are usually 'judgers' and have more awareness of time.

- ❧ Modal Operator Sequence – This is the motivational driver for individuals and will indicate how they will apply themselves to a task. Necessity will use language like *must, try, got to, have to*, Possibility will use language like *could, can, would*.

- ❧ Attention Direction – This is where one places one's attention. Self places the attention on themselves first, others places their attention on other people first.

Communication Preference

- ❧ Information Processing Style – External processors need to go external to make sense of their information. They may only want you to listen and not give advice. Internal will process their information internally.

- ❧ Listening Style – Individuals will listen Literally where they only hear the literal things that you say. Inferential listeners will infer things from the communication that you offer.

- ❧ Speaking Style – Similar to the listening style, speakers will be inferential or literal. Inferential speakers will infer things in their speech without saying it outright whereas literal speakers will say it as it is.

Process and procedure of Metaprogrammes

Each metaprogramme has a question to elicit it and these are given below along with examples of responses from the range of options.

Simple Metaprogrammes Elicitation

- ❧ Introvert/Extrovert – *'When it is time to recharge your batteries, do you prefer to be alone or with people?'*. An introvert will prefer to be alone, and extrovert will prefer to be with people.

- ❧ Sensor/Intuitor – *'If we were going to study a certain subject, which would you be more interested in knowing: the facts and their utility right now (Sensor), or the ideas and the relationships between the ideas and their use in the future?'*. (Intuitor)

- ❧ Thinker/Feeler – *'Is it more important for you to be thought of as a fair/caring/sensitive person (feeler), or a reasonable/logical/objective person?'* (thinker) or *'When you make a decision, do you rely more on impersonal reason and logic (thinker), or more on personal values?'*. (feeler)

ଈ Judger/Perceiver – *'If we were going to do a project together, would you prefer that it were outlined, planned and orderly (judger), or would you prefer that we were able to be more flexible in the project?'. (perceiver)*

Complex Metaprogrammes Elicitation

Each of the metaprogrammes are summarised here with a description of what they portray.

ଈ Direction Filter – *'What do you want in a car (job/relationship)?'* or *'What's important to you about _____?'*. This is similar to the process in values explained earlier in the chapter. Influencing language - Toward: *Get attain, achieve have, attract, include, obtain.* Away From: *Avoid, repulsed by, steer clear of, keep away from, exclude, get rid of, not have.*

ଈ Reason Filter – *'Why did you choose your current job?'* Influencing language - Options: *Possibilities, choices, options, reasons, other ways, alternatives, why to.* Procedures: *Procedure, right way, proven way, only way, known way. Correct way, how to.*

ଈ Frame of reference – *'How do you know when you're doing a good job?'* Influencing Language - Internal: *Only you can decide, it is up to you* External: *Other people think the facts show, this is the way it is, here is some feedback.*

ଈ Convincer Representational Filter – *'How do you know when someone else is good at what they do?* Influencing language - Looks right: *See, look, picture, envision, clear, sight;* Sounds right: *Hear, listen, sounds right;* Feels right: *Do, feel, touch, experience;* Makes sense: *Sense, reason, facts, data read, documentation instructions.*

ଈ Convincer Demonstration Filter – *'How often does someone have to demonstrate competence to you before you're convinced?'*. Influencing Language - Automatic: (There is no need to convince this person, they will be, automatically); Consistent: *'I know you will never be completely convinced, and that's the reason why you'll have to do this to find out'*; A Number of Times: *'Here are _____ (a number of) options. I'm sure that you will find one of them is right for you'*; One Time: *'Here is the option which makes the most sense'*; and, A Period of Time: (Call the person in a period of time which is no less than 10% of the total period of time, and say:) *'I've been so busy since the last time we talked, it almost seems like _____ (total period)'.*

∞ Management Direction Filter – There are 3 questions for this filter (i)'*Do you know what you need to do to be successful at your job?*'; (ii) '*Do you know what someone else needs to do to be successful at their job?*'; and, (iii) '*Are you willing to tell them?*'. Self and Others (Yes, Yes, Yes): Known as managers, they know what needs to be done, what you need to do and are willing to give you directions. Self Only (Yes, No, Yes): '*You know that what other people do in this project is not important to you, and that is why…*'. Others Only (No, Yes, Yes): '*The boss knows what we need to do, so that's why we should…*': and, Self but Not Others (Yes, Yes, No): '*Who are we to tell them what to do? But that's why we must*'.

∞ Action Filter – '*When you come into a situation do you usually act quickly after sizing it up* (proactive), *or do you do a complete study of all the consequences and then act?*(reactive)' Influencing language – Proactive: no language required, they just do it; Both: '*You've had all the time you need to study this, and now is the time for action*'; Active: '*Let's go and do this project. There's no need to wait*'; and, Reflective: '*I know you want to study this. It's OK. Take all the time you need to make the decision now*'.

∞ Work Style or Affiliation Filter – '*Tell me about a work situation in which you were the happiest, a one-time event.*' Independent player uses lots of 'I' language, a Management player uses lots of 'I' and 'We' language, a team player uses lots of 'We' language in their responses. Influencing language - Independent Player: '*You have a high need to be independent, and that is why it is important to foster teamwork in this situation*'; Management Player: '*I know you want to be in charge…*'; and, Team Player: '*I know that you want a team to play with…*'.

∞ Work Preference Filter or Organisational Sort – '*Tell me about a work situation in which you were the happiest, a one-time event.*' A people preference will tell you about the people, a things preference will tell you about the things that they were working with or on, and, a systems preference will tell you about the wider system. Influencing Language - People: '*Let me tell you about the people who will be working on this project*'; Things: '*Let me tell you about what we'll be working with*'; and, Systems: '*Let me tell you how the system works*'.

∞ Primary Interest Filter – '*What's your favourite restaurant? Tell me about it.*' A People preference will tell you who they are with. A Place preference will tell you about the geography or location. A Things preference will tell you about things like the theme or food. An Activity preference will tell you about what was going on. An Information preference will ask you 'why' and then respond to your reason. Influencing language – People: *'Let me tell you who you will be working with on this project'*; Place: *'Let me tell you where this project is ...'*; Things: *'Let me tell you what we'll need'*; Activity: *'Let me tell you how this will work'*; and, Information: *'Let me tell you what you need to know, and why'*.

    ❧ Chunk Size Filter – *'If we were going to do a project together, would you want to know the big picture first* (Global), *or the details first* (Specific). *Would you really need to know the...* (ask other)? If they prefer big picture and need detail they are global to specific, if they prefer specific and they need the big picture, they are specific to global. Influencing language - Global: *'Here's the big picture...'* (Don't give too many details, stay abstract); Global to Specific: *'Here's the big picture... now here are the details'*; Specific: *'Here are the details'* (Be specific. Don't use abstractions); Specific to Global: *'Here are the details...and here's the big picture'*.

    ❧ Relationship Filter – *'What is the relationship between what you're doing this year and what you did at this time last year?'* Sameness – they will discuss same or common features or will say *'They are the same'*; Sameness with Exception – they will mention similarities first and then the difference *'Better, more, less'*; Sameness and Differences Equally - Predominantly comparisons *'It's busier'*; Differences with Exception - Differences and then similarities; Differences - Things are totally different *'New, changed, revolutionary'*. Influencing language - Differences: *'You probably won't believe this...'*; Difference with Exception: *'I don't know if you will believe this or not...'* ; Sameness: *'This is the same as what you already know (or "are doing")'*; Sameness with Exception: *'As you consider what I've said you'll find it is the same as what you already know. Then as you consider it, you will probably find the reasons why it's different, and those are the reasons why you will want to do it'*.

    ❧ Emotional Stress Response – *'Tell me about a situation* (context-related) *that gave you trouble, a one-time event.'* (Observe eye accessing). Thinking will have no feeling and will respond from Ad (auditory digital) language. Choice will respond in feeling and then immediately go to thinking to reassess the situation. Feeling will stay in feeling and may even get upset. Influencing Language - Thinking: *'I know that this situation doesn't upset you at all, and perhaps you need to show some feeling in this situation'*; Feeling: *'I know this situation upsets you, but...'*; Choice: *'You have the choice to react or not in this situation…'*.

- Time Storage Filter – 'What direction is the past and what direction is the future for you?' Influencing language - In Time: *'You know that we are apt to lose track of time, so let's keep track of what time it is'* or. *'Keeping our options open';* Through Time: *'Time is of the essence, as you know, so let's...'* or, *'Let's take this step by step'.*

- Modal Operator Sequence – *'What was the last thing you said to yourself just before you got out of bed this morning'* Influencing language: Use their modal operator in sentences, e.g. *'you could think about this'* or, *'you must see how this is possible'.*

- Attention Direction – No question, just observe their responses to an event, e.g. a cup spilling on the floor or someone sneezing. Self: Minimal eye contact. Sits by self. Makes assumptions based on internal thoughts and feelings. Others: Make assumptions based on other peoples reactions.

Communication Preference

- Information Processing Style – *'When you need to work through a problem or a challenge in your life, is it absolutely necessary for you to: Talk about it with someone else* (external), *or Think about it by yourself only* (internal)?

- Listening Style – *'If someone you knew quite well said to you, "I'm thirsty," would you: Find the comment interesting, but probably do nothing about it* (literal), *or would you feel really compelled to do something about it?* (inferential).

- Speaking Style – *'If you felt that someone around you was not performing as well as they should, would you: Come to the point and tell them directly* (literal), *or would you Hint, imply and give them clues'* (inferential).

Exercise

Complete the following metaprogramme question sheet for yourself.

1. Direction Sort:

What do you want in a job?

- or - What do you want in a relationship?
- or - What do you want in a car?
- or - What do you want to do with your life?
- or – For you, what's important about what you do?

    (If problems, elicit complex equivalence, next page.)

☐ Toward
☐ T/A
☐ Both
☐ A/T
☐ Away from

2. Options/Procedures:

Why are you choosing to do what you're doing?

☐Possibility
☐Necessity

3. Frame of Reference:

How do you know when you've done a good job?

(Do you just know insider or does someone have to tell you?)

☐Internal
☐External
☐I/Check

4. Convincer (Representational):

How do you know that a co-worker is good at his/her job?

☐See
☐Hear
☐Do
☐Read

5. Convincer (Demonstration):

How often does a co-worker have to demonstrate competence to you before you are convinced?

☐Automatic
☐ ____ Time(s)
☐Consistent
☐Period of time

6. Management Direction Filter:

a. Do you know what you need to do to increase your chances for success on a job?

b. Do you know a good way for someone else to increase their chances?

c. Do you find it easy to tell them, or not so easy?

☐Self & Others
☐Self only
☐Others only
☐Self but not others

7. Action Level Sort:

When you come into a situation, do you usually act quickly after sizing it up, or do you do a detailed study of all the consequences and then act?

☐Active
☐Reflective
☐Both
☐Inactive

8,9. Tell me about a work situation in which you were the happiest.

(A one time event)

_____

_____

_____

_____

_____

_____

_____

AFFILIATION FILTER:

☐Independent
☐Management
☐Team

_____ **WORK**
_____ **PREFERENCE**
_____ **FILTER:**
_____ ☐Things
_____ ☐People
_____ ☐Systems
_____
_____

10. Tell me about your favourite restaurant?

_____ **PRIMARY**
_____ **INTEREST**
_____ **FILTER:**
_____ ☐People
_____ ☐Places
_____ ☐Things
_____ ☐Activity
_____ ☐Information

11. Chunk Size   ☐Global>Specific

If we were going to do a project together, would you   ☐Specific>Global
want to know all the details first or the big picture first? ☐Global
Would you really need to know the *(ask opposite)* big   ☐Specific
picture/ details?

12. Relationship Sort:

(Use the boxes or one of the questions below)   ☐Sameness

What's the relationship between what you're doing   ☐Sameness with
this year, and what you were doing last year?   exception

                                                         ☐Sameness and
_____   differences equally
_____   ☐Differences
_____   with exception
_____   ☐Differences

- or –   When you come into a new situation,
do you usually notice the similarities or the
differences first?

_____

_____

_____

_____

13. Emotional Stress Response:

Tell me about a work situation that gave you trouble

☐Thinking
☐Feeling
☐Chioce

_____

_____

_____

_____

_____

_____

14. Time Storage:

☐In time F/B
☐Through time L/R

What I'd like to ask you to do is STOP, and relax.
And recall a memory from the past *(future)*. Now will you
please point to where in space the memory came from?

*(To check, ask if they care if someone's
late for an appointment.)*

15. Modal Operator Sequence:

How did you get up this morning?   _____

What did you say to yourself?   _____

(can, must, have to, want to, got to, should, etc.)

16. Attention Direction:

☐Self
☐Others
☐Both

17. Information Processing Style

When you need to work through a problem or a challenge
in your life, is it absolutely necessary for you to:

☐Internal
☐External

Talk about it with someone else, or

Think about it by yourself only?

18. Listening Style

If someone you knew quite well said to you, "I'm thirsty," would you:

☐ Inferential
☐ Literal

Find the comment interesting, but probably do nothing about it or

would you feel really compelled to do something about it?

19. Speaking Style

If you felt that someone around you was not performing as well as they should, would you:

☐ Inferential
☐ Literal

Come to the point and tell them directly, or

would you **Hint, imply and give them clues'**

Applications

Coaching – Enabling a coachee to understand and work with their own and others information processing styles.

Recruitment – Advertise and recruit against a specific metaprogramme profile.

Education – Utilise an understanding of metaprogrammes to assist students/ learners develop effective learning strategies using their existing preferences.

Personal relationships – Share an understanding of each others preferences and adapt your behaviour so that information and decisions are made according to individual preferences.

> Think like a wise man but
> communicate in the language
> of other people.
>
> W.B. Yeats

Chapter Eleven

Performance Excellence

Perfecting your skills

NLP IS a psychology of performance excellence and as has been demonstrated in the previous chapters, all of the tools, techniques and principles of NLP have been developed from modelling excellence in diverse contexts. Although originally modelled from therapists, NLP has gone on to model from behaviourists, linguists, computer programming, sports, education, and neuroscience. It is important to remember that within NLP, it was the outputs that were initially modelled from the work of Satir, Perls and Erickson by Bandler and Grinder rather than the specific strategies, beliefs and values that influenced the therapists.

Pareto's (1935) principle that, "80% of results are produced by 20% of people", also applies to the modelling process within NLP. 80% of what you achieve is based on 20% of your input. The challenge is – what are those people doing differently to get the results and what are the 80% doing that if you were to change it would make a difference?

 This chapter reviews the **modelling** process of NLP.

Modelling

Modelling within NLP assumes that given a specific behaviour, ability or skill that an individual can perform, one can replicate that behaviour (ability or skill) in half the time it took to teach the skill originally. We start with the idea that all people are equal in terms of physical and mental capabilities. The only differences are the issues of motivation – values, beliefs, attitudes - which can drive one to be excellent (an independent variable in the training function) – either towards or away from as the motivation force.

Rationale

Modelling as a process within NLP begins with the presupposition that *If One Person Can Do It, Anybody Can*. Some of the components within NLP that make modelling possible are: Rapport and Attentiveness – the more you gain rapport with someone, the more likely it is that they will trust you and share with you their conscious and unconscious strategies for their successful behaviour; an Attitude of Curiosity and Learning – one of the fundamental principles of NLP; the Identifying of Patterns and Sequences; breaking down the patterns and sequences into their Constituents and Parts; Modelling effective patterns.

Bodenhamer and Hall (1999) define modelling as 'the process of observing and replicating the successful actions and behaviours of others; the process of discerning the sequence of internal representations that enable someone to accomplish the task' (p 395).

Evidence base

Swets et al (1990) in their critical review of NLP techniques being adopted by the US army did suggest that there was some effectiveness and future study potential in the modelling of motor skill techniques. Sparrow (2006) proposes that the NLP process of modelling is a powerful tool for Human Resource personnel to enable an understanding of human behaviour.

Principles of modelling

Modelling enables us to:

- ❧ Reduce training time
- ❧ Reach a higher level of expertise
- ❧ Pre-select – hire those with talent and innate ability
- ❧ Design the man/machine interface so that it is useful
- ❧ Get better at something yourself and then install behaviour in self.

There are two main principles to modelling within NLP. The first principle is to utilise Isomorphic Modelling which involves taking what an expert is doing and installing it in others, which can significantly accelerate training times. Generative Modelling which involves working with a model to enable them to develop their model to even greater performance. This can be used in sports performance, behavioural based coaching, management and leadership programmes and therapy contexts.

Modelling works by de-nominalising or chunking down the key elements or steps to find the processes for a specific behaviour.

There are a number of approaches to modelling in the wider perspective of understanding human behaviour. These patterns of modelling are demonstrated in the figure below.

Patterns of modelling

„ **Science Behaviourism** is based on the principles of modelling found in the work of John Grinder. It involves clear focus on the process and stays at structure and process level rather than paying attention to the content of the story.

„ **Systems/Sociology** is based on the systemic perspectives of Behr and Aycoffe. It considers the interconnections within a system and measures behaviour from an 'outside the system' perspective. The principle of systemic modelling assumes that the individual can only change if the system changes.

- Culture/Anthropology involves modelling of ethics and values. The modeller immerses themselves in the culture. Change occurs through the culture.

- Psychology/Art is a dialogical process of modelling. It is used within psychotherapy to model more useful internal states and processes and within business as emotional intelligence. Modelling is focussed on the individual and supports empowerment of the individual.

Process of modelling

There are 2 processes that are used for modelling.

- Inside Modelling. This process involves conscious and unconscious imitation of the Model. The 80/20 rule applies here and rather than determine the 20% that makes the difference at the outset, the model is imitated and then various elements are dropped to identify the critical elements of the model.

- Outside Modelling. This process is more time consuming, however, it results in a more accurate model. The model is identified initially and the key components of the task laid out. Literature is reviewed and considered to see if it supports the model. Between 4-6 experts are modelled and 3 contrast models are also looked at to determine what the expert does that the contrast does not do. A provisional model is developed and then tested. Once the model is refined, it is trained and installed in others.

Modelling can involve a number of different attributes.

- Physical modelling – such as gross muscle movements used in excellent sports performance

- Emotional modelling – in successful individuals, and in certain careers such as those by Goldman who modelled the strategies of bomb disposal teams.

- Mental modelling – to understand and refine intellectual skill. Mental operation processes such as morse code training, mental arithmetic, artificial intelligence. It can also be used to understand creative processes such as those found in business entrepreneurs.

- Social modelling – of cultures to understand cultural norms and changes in society

- Spiritual modelling – such as faith healers, miracle workers.

Procedure for modelling

There are 5 steps to the modelling procedure.

ಸಿ Setting the framework for extraction

What types of problems do experts experience when they are performing the skill?

What skills and knowledge are required to resolve problems?

What are the major components of the task?

What are the underlying skills in performing the task?

What is the underlying motivation?

What mental and/or physical steps occur when faced with certain conditions?

How does the model choose among multiple actions or consequences to actions?

What challenges do novices face?

Which skills/knowledge should be transferred to the trainees?

ಸಿ Framework for Extraction

Which aspects of the experts performance will be modelled?

What constraints are there on access to the model, e.g. time, environment, training?

How will you structure your extraction process e.g. what is your outcome?

Develop a process to understand metaprogrammes, large skill chunks, strategies, practical demonstration, scenarios, refinement of the model.

ಸಿ Extraction Methods

Structured and unstructured interviews

Direct observation and skill analysis

Skill refinement.

๛ Elicitation of Model

Outcome

Assumptions   Hours of influence: the longer you are with them the more you will learn

People like to talk more than they listen

People like to talk about themselves

Show genuine interest in the person

Be willing to share your information

The more you listen the more you will have control of the interaction.

Calibrate   The environment

Feedback

All behaviour has meaning.

๛ Model Synthesis

Elicit the components

Identify the critical components by looking at variables, boundaries or constraints, patterns

Prune and reduce components

Develop critical knowledge base

Develop the hierarchy or the structure of the model

Test and refine the model

Teach to others.

Modelling Processes

Exercise

A simple modelling exercise is a useful place to start to understand the modelling process for people.

Find 2 colleagues to work with.

Have one person walk a short distance – 10 metres or so.

A second person copies the walk.

The observer person acts as a coach making suggestions on which elements of the walking could change to match the first person.

Applications

Coaching – Model out successful strategies and transfer these to other contexts.

Sports performance – Model excellence in a sport and use this as a protocol for training novices in the sport.

Business performance – Identify an out-performing unit or team within the business. Model their strategies for performance and introduce these to lesser performing areas.

The noblest search is the
search for excellence.

Lyndon B. Johnson

Chapter Twelve

NLP: Principles in Practice

THE HISTORY of NLP began in 1976 and since then there have been significant advances in neuroscience, cognitive linguistics, coaching practice and understanding the dimensions of human relationships. Yet much of the map of NLP remains unchanged other than distortions, deletions and generalisations that have occurred as the story has been passed down through three generations. At this point in time there is an increase across the spectrum of applications and approaches to NLP. This can be seen as sitting along a continuum from the traditional trainers and practitioners who adhere to the roots of NLP as it was taught to them and those trainers and practitioners who are evidencing their work, using this evidence to question some of the assumptions of the power and/or applicability of some of the techniques and who are moving their training and practice alongside or into recognised and in some instances legally inferred institutions such as Universities.

NLP in higher education

Within the UK NLP is now being taught and studied as part of mainstream higher education. Kingston University includes NLP as a core component of its MA in Supervision, Mentoring and Coaching. This programme developed out of an MA in Coaching and NLP which has its historical roots initiated at Portsmouth University by Sally Vanson, who developed and ran the world's first Masters degree in NLP. Surrey University Management School have a number of students studying their Doctorates in NLP with some already being awarded a PhD in this area.

Other programmes such as those offered by Leeds Metropolitan University provide post graduate leadership degrees that include a significant component of

NLP. Middlesex University incorporate NLP into their Sports Psychology degrees. The Universities of Salford and Teesside have supported students to complete Masters degrees in Counselling, Psychotherapy and Advanced Clinical Practice by granting Accreditation for Prior Learning in NLP programmes and studies that have focussed specifically on NLP as a therapy.

I have been unable to source any higher education degrees across the rest of Europe that include significant elements of NLP or where NLP is the primary focus of study.

I have been unable to source any existing higher education degrees in the United States that are specifically focussed towards NLP. There are three University linked activities that are providing substantial links into the higher education system in the US through extensive research and development programmes. These are summarised below.

The NLP University *www.nlpu.com* operates from the University of California Campus and was set up by Robert Dilts and Todd Epstein in 1991. The University offers a graduate studies programme. Although the programmes do not lead to higher education awards the focus of NLPU is to provide a community context whereby the global potential of Systemic NLP can be considered through the research and development of new tools and technologies.

The NLP Research and Recognition *www.nlprandr.org* project has been developed in the United States, spearheaded by Frank Bourke and supported by Judith DeLozier and Steve and Connirae Andreas as Trustees. The project is an independent not-for-profit organisation with the aim of advancing the science of NLP through funded programmes of research. The project is linked to Marshall University, West Virginia, where a training site for the clinical practice of NLP in managing Post Traumatic Stress Disorder is being developed. This is the first recognition of NLP within a department at an American University.

The project lists its aims as:

- ⁖ To develop, support and communicate the development of research which serve to provide basic scientific validity for NLP and allied techniques as well as the continued refinement and development of such techniques in the U.S. and abroad

- ⁖ To establish NLP treatment centres of excellence for certain "diseases" such as asthma, phobias, anxiety disorders, post traumatic stress, depression, etc. as well as adjunctive health aids

- To identify professionally approved academic programs, here and abroad, in Clinical Psychology, Psychiatry, Social Work and allied mental health fields and work with them to integrate NLP and allied methodology into their practice
- To develop continuing educational credits for learning NLP and allied clinical skills for the National Professional Organizations of Psychiatry, Psychology, Social Work, etc.
- To Develop University and Hospital based clearing houses for the evaluation of utilization protocols, here and abroad
- To develop the economic and organisational resources to continue to accomplish these goals for a long term future.

The above project was supported through the Institute for the Advanced Studies of Health, *www.nlpiash.org*. IASH is run by 4 well known members of the NLP community, Robert Dilts, Tim Hallbom, Suzi Smith and Steve Andreas. The aim of the project is to sponsor excellence in NLP for the wellbeing of the world's people and the health of all systems. IASH has a three-fold mission:

- To identify and support NLP research projects that study health and well-being for individuals, groups and organisations
- To promote and support a sustainable NLP community dedicated to their vision and values
- To create avenues of communication which attract, educate and motivate people to apply NLP in their lives.

Australia has a number of higher education institutions that recognise and endorse NLP training that meets the requirements of the government's competency based training standards, enabling NLP programmes to be considered as part or all of a postgraduate diploma or degree. (Linder-Pelz, 2010 pp.56).

Professional associations

There are a number of bodies that operate as professional associations for NLP. The UK has five such associations, ANLP (Association for NLP), British Board of NLP, International Neurolinguistic Programming Trainers Association (INLPTA) and the Professional Guild of NLP and for therapy, The Neurolinguistic Psychotherapy and Counselling Association (NLPtCA). Each of the following descriptions is taken from the respective websites, the public face of each organisation on 1 March 2010.

ANLP (Association for NLP) *www.anlp.org* is a Social Enterprise (Community Interest Company) and is the only independent NLP organisation in the UK and is not directly linked to any training organisation. ANLP's aim is to represent an impartial and independent voice for NLP and create a spirit of unity and co-operation while abiding by the philosophy and presuppositions of NLP. ANLP maintains standards and encourages best practice in the community as well as informing the public about the benefits and applications of NLP. ANLP has a stated code of ethics and all members are required to adhere to this code. The organisation is supported by a number of Fellows: Steve and Connirae Andreas, Judith DeLozier, Robert Dilts, Charles Faulkner, Steve Gilligan, Christina Hall, Bill O'Hanlon and Wyatt Woodsmall. ANLP lists an Advisory Board consisting of Nick Kemp, Jeremy Lazarus, Judith Lowe, John Seymour, David Shephard, Emily Terry and Lisa Wake.

ANLP also has global links and is developing standards and a platform in other European countries.

The British Board of NLP *www.bbnlp.com* operates as an NLP community that provides member benefits with a primary focus on supporting those with NLP qualifications in creating and growing therapeutic and coaching businesses. The organisation has direct links to training companies and is not independent from them, with both Directors being Trainers of NLP. It lists combined aims with its training company as wanting to see:

- Widespread acceptance of NLP as a viable therapeutic discipline and a credible means of facilitating change
- Development of research into, and applications of, NLP for the benefit of humanity
- Partnership and compatibility among the many training centres and coaching schools offering NLP training
- Constant improvement in NLP's professional standards
- A culture of respect, sharing and mutual support within the NLP community.

It states that its aim is to support those who are qualified in NLP to create or improve their existing business and to unite potential clients with qualified practitioners of NLP and other related therapies. The organisation does not appear to list a code of ethics on its website, neither does it adhere to the quasi-regulatory components that are required for those individuals who wish to practice psychological based therapies.

BBNLP lists its advisory panel consisting of Steve Andreas, Michael Beale, Shelle Rose Charvet, Robert Dilts, Charles Faulkner, Tad James, James Lawley, Ian McDermott, Penny Tomkins.

Professional Associations

The International NLP Trainers Association, *www.inlpta.co.uk*, is linked to Wyatt Woodsmall and is an international co-operative association of aligned NLP Trainers and Master Trainers who have agreed to abide by and uphold INLPTA's standards of quality, professionalism and ethics in their NLP accreditation training and in the conduct of their NLP business. INLPTA lists clear criteria for membership and Trainers are required to teach core content over a minimum number of hours of face to face teaching. INLPTA also lists a code of ethics. The organisation also has global links and has its head office in America.

The Professional Guild of NLP, *www.professionalguildofnlp.com*, is a like-minded professional NLP Training Organisation that is non commercial and not for profit. It has direct links to one training school and states independence of any one school, lead trainer or mindset. The Guild seeks to provide an interface between quality NLP training and the public. The Guild was set up in 2003 by a group of Founder Members who were committed to maintaining the original provision of a minimum of 120 hours of direct training in no less than 18 days, providing supervised practice of skills learnt. The Guild is committed to forward thinking development and provides a progression route for qualified NLP Trainers to establish their own business as a bona fide recognised NLP Training Organisation.

The Neurolinguistic Psychotherapy and Counselling Association, *www.nlptca.com* is a not-for-profit company that is dedicated to developing and promoting the use of NLP in therapeutic and counselling settings. NLPtCA officers are elected by the membership and it operates a code of conduct, ethics and practice.

The organisation exists to:

- Develop and maintain standards for the practice of Neuro-Linguistic Psychotherapy and Counselling interests

- Monitor the activities and further the interests of its members

- Represent the interests of NLPtCA to other professional and regulatory authorities engaged in the field of psychotherapy and counselling

- Promote Neuro-Linguistic Psychotherapy and Counselling to a wider public and to further the use of the techniques, training and practice of NLPt in personal development.

NLPtCA is a Member Organisation of the United Kingdom Council for Psychotherapy (UKCP).

Professional body recognition

Within the UK there are three quasi regulatory bodies that have some authority over NLP as it is applied in specific contexts.

The Chartered Institute for Personnel and Development, *www.cipd. co.uk*, is Europe's largest professional body for HR personnel. The aim of CIPD is to drive sustained organisation performance through HR, shaping thinking, leading practice and building capability within the professions. It works closely with Sue Knight to provide short courses in the applications of NLP in the HR context.

The Institute of Leadership and Management, *www.i-l-m.com*, exists to support, develop and inform managers through their careers. The organisation includes NLP within its leadership and management training as a recognised communications tool and some training schools are being granted level 7 accreditation with ILM for their practitioner and master practitioner programmes.

The United Kingdom Council for Psychotherapy (UKCP) *www. psychotherapy.org.uk* is a psychotherapy umbrella organisation that has agreed national standards for approaches to psychotherapy. Within UKCP there are now three bodies that represent NLPt (Neurolinguistic Psychotherapy): NLPtCA as an accrediting and membership organisation; Awaken School of Outcome Oriented Psychotherapies *www.awakenschool.co.uk*; and BeeLeaf Institute for Contemporary Psychotherapy, *www.beeleaf.com*, both as training and accrediting organisations. NLP as a psychotherapy is represented in Europe through EANLPt (European Association for Neurolingusitic Psychotherapy) *www.eanlpt.org* which is a Member Organisation of the European Association for Psychotherapy.

Regulation of psychological professions

There are a number of regulatory processes occurring that have implications for NLP and NLP practice in the UK.

The UK Government has been working for the last few years on the regulation of the psychological professions. This has resulted in the statutory regulation of Psychology via the Health Professions Council (HPC) in July 2009. Two voluntary registers were transferred to the HPC with all 15,000 members on the Register regulated under the HPC. These registers were the ones maintained by the British Psychological Society (BPS) and the Association of Educational Psychologists (AEP). The HPC has utilised the title *Practitioner Psychologist* and identifies psychology as *the scientific study of people, the mind and behaviour. Psychologists attempt to understand the role of mental functions in individual and social behaviour.* There are 9 protected titles: Clinical Psychologist, Counselling Psychologist, Educational Psychologist, Forensic Psychologist, Health Psychologist, Occupational Psychologist, Practitioner Psychologist, Registered Psychologist, and, Sport and Exercise Psychologist. Under these titles are 7 domains of practice: Clinical Psychologists, Counselling Psychologists, Educational Psychologists, Forensic Psychologists, Health Psychologists, Occupational Psychologists, and, Sport and Exercise Psychologists.

In 2007, the Government published a White Paper, *'Trust, Assurance and Safety – The Regulation of Health Professionals in the 21st Century'*. This paper made recommendations on the regulation of Psychotherapists and Counsellors as a priority group. The HPC are currently consulting on the recommendations that include the structure of the Register, protected titles, voluntary register transfer and grandparenting arrangements (the process whereby existing practitioners who are not currently registered with one of the voluntary registers is assessed for levels of competence and brought into the regulatory system), standards of education and training and standards of proficiency. The results of this consultation was reported in December 2009 and concluded that as Psychologists are now subject to statutory regulation there are some implications for psychotherapy and counselling and that the regulation of psychologists may be used as building blocks to meet the regulatory needs of psychotherapists and counsellors. The recommendations suggest that standards of proficiency need to be developed before it is clear whether it is possible to differentiate between psychotherapists and counsellors. They also suggest that the differentiation that exists between modalities of therapy could not be addressed through different titles as it would be confusing for the public and it may also negatively impact on the inclusivity of practitioners and diversity of practice. However Registrants would be able to use preceding adjectives before the protected title to indicate their orientation of practice. There is an overall recommendation that the titles of Psychotherapist and Counsellor should be protected titles. This includes the use of the title by other professions e.g. if someone is a nurse or doctor or other regulated professional and they wish to practice as a psychotherapist or counsellor, they would need to hold dual registration. Recommendations have also been made regarding grandparenting for those individuals who are currently practicing and who may not be on one of the existing recognised voluntary registers. Recommendations are that grandparenting should only be available for 3 years.

Across Europe there are a number of countries where psychotherapy is a state regulated activity and within this falls the activity of NLP as a therapeutic discipline. Further information can be obtained from EANLPt, *www.eanlpt.org*.

Coaching and NLP

Coaching is increasingly becoming recognised as a medium for change with NLP forming a substantial part of the toolkit for many coaches. Linder-Pelz (2010) has considered the evidence based approach for using NLP in Coaching and provides an excellent exposition of the distinguishing features of NLP coaching that sets it apart from other cognitive behavioural or solution focussed approaches (2010 p.100). Linder-Pelz reports Mathison's research into NLP and coaching as the first that tested the model of and assumptions about the language patterns of NLP and how they can be used to influence beliefs, internal representations and responses (2010 p.106-107). Vanson is also quoted by Linder-Pelz and her study on the use of coaching in a promotion process (p.107).

There are a number of voluntary regulatory bodies for coaching globally. These include the Association for Coaching *www.associationforcoaching.com;* the International Coach Federation, *www.coachfederation.org;* and, European Coaching and Mentoring Council, *www.emccouncil.org*. Each of these bodies recognises NLP based coaching as an accepted model of coaching.

There are a few new developments in the coaching community that have emerged from NLP. Michael Hall (1995/2000) has developed Neuro-Semantics as a coaching model through his understanding of NLP and other positive psychology approaches. The approach is designed to facilitate actualisation of highest and best performance that is based on personal values and ethics.

Business and NLP

There are a multitude of NLP training and consultancy practices that provide NLP based interventions into the business world. Many of these are successful and some less so. I have worked with businesses since 1997 applying NLP in a number of different ways and in recent years it has become more acceptable to bring NLP in as a mainstream topic rather than disguising it as something else such as communication skills, sales based training etc. There is still a lack of evidence base for NLP in the business sector and where research does exist I have endeavoured to include it in the relevant section in this book.

Education and NLP

Churches and West-Burnham (2009) have been supporting the Children's Agenda in England with their work on NLP with the CfBT Education Trust, *www. CfBT.com*. The DfES (Department for Education and Skills) and subsequently the NCSL (National College for School Leadership) have worked closely with the CfBT for the provision of training and professional development for teachers. The Fast Track teaching programme has enabled the delivery of a number of training programmes for several thousand teachers including *NLP for Teacher and School Leaders, Coaching for Leadership, Making it Happen, Authentic Leadership,* and *Getting Your Life Back.*

Therapy and NLP

Neurolinguistic psychotherapy (NLPt) emerged from the early modelling of the linguistic patterns of Erickson, Satir and Perls by the co-founders of Neurolinguistic Programming (NLP) Bandler and Grinder. In the mid 1980's, therapists in the UK became interested in NLP and it's application in the therapy field. By 1996, a formal therapy body for NLPt developed as an off-shoot to the Association of NLP. Therapists McDermott and Jago (2001), Lawley and Tomkins (2005), Gawler-Wright (1999, 2006), and Wake (2008) began to integrate the application of NLP in therapeutic work, such that it is now recognised as a brief psychotherapy.

There is increasing evidence for the effectiveness of NLPt as a psychotherapy and these have been included in this book where relevant.

Sports and NLP

NLP is being used more widely within the sporting arena and books such as Lazarus' *Ahead of the Game* are making it more accessible to sports coaches and participants. NLP provides an applied psychology approach to Sports and enables the combination of performance excellence and a winning mind set. It is widely known that some of the top sports performers in the UK and America have used NLP coaches to maximise their performance and although there is anecdotal evidence of its effectiveness there is limited empirical evidence.

Health care and NLP

There are only a few books that discuss the applications of NLP in a health care context. Walker (2004) has written a highly accessible book on the applications of NLP in medical practice from his perspective as a General Practitioner. He provides an excellent context of the applications and makes suggestions on how NLP can be used to manage clinical disorders such as depression, anxiety, habit disorders, pain control and cancer. He links NLP to other psychotherapeutic approaches and also addresses some concerns in his chapter on 'the dark side of the force' where he challenges some of the assumptions that are taught in some schools of NLP and what he sees as some inherent dangers.

Henwood and Lister (2007) look at the use of NLP and Coaching for Health Care Professionals, providing a tool kit based approach to managing in a professional environment.

Where next for NLP?

The recent book by Tosey and Mathison (2009): *Neurolinguistic Programming. A Critical Appreciation for Managers and Developers* has provided a much needed review and reflection on the status of NLP. Additionally the publication of the proceedings from the First International NLP Research Conference in 2009 has placed a marker in the sand to move NLP forward by individuals who want to see NLP grounded in empirical evidence.

Tosey and Mathison (p.189-195) suggest that the future of NLP holds 3 potential scenarios.

1. Entropy where the energy that has driven NLP this far forward dissipates and disorder arises. Tosey and Mathison suggest that this is already occurring as much of what is taught in NLP is the recycling of the original material, with

very little new material or understanding being developed. In my experience of developing this book it is clear that there are new thoughts and ideas being developed. In reading some of the evidence as I have researched material for this book, there are some excellent findings and recommendations from research studies, yet there are almost no occasions where these are followed through by the author and published in a later work.

2. Seeds of its own destruction which may result from the increasing diversity of opinion that is occurring in the field. Tosey and Mathison refer to the divisions in the field that have emerged through the different approaches to training, whether it is those who follow the 7 day accelerated course model, those who have a kinship with Bandler, or who pursue the more philosophical approach of Grinder and I would add in those who are pursuing a more academic base to their work. Statutory regulation across Europe is placing pressure on the community, and in the UK there are only very limited numbers of practitioners who place themselves with one of the voluntary bodies for regulation. Tosey and Mathison also suggest that emerging fields such as neuroscience may over take NLP as it can provide the empirical evidence base to support its theories.

3. Renaissance where the field embraces new and emerging theories and acts as a complementary tool kit and knowledge base for other practices. Tosey and Mathison suggest that for this to happen the NLP community needs to become familiar with research and begin to question its efficacy.

Summary

NLP is a growing and developing field. Recent advances in neuroscience and cognitive linguistics have provided an ideal opportunity for NLP to demonstrate the effectiveness of its approach, with researchers and authors in human development, cognitive linguistics and neuroscience beginning to demonstrate some of what NLP has had as a fundamental theory for over 30 years. The field has a number of choices open to it. It can continue to grow at a rate of speed, with more and more individuals being trained in NLP in its traditional format, with each training adding further dilution to the field. Like any approach there is a spectrum to the effectiveness of this training. Some of it is excellent, some is ok and fit for purpose and some consists of misrepresentations, flaws and errors.

There still exists a perception that NLP is a cult, or that trainers attract 'groupies' who want to have some of the shine rub off on them.

Some businesses, HR professionals, educators, therapists and psychologically minded individuals do not take NLP seriously.

For NLP to experience the renaissance suggested by Tosey and Mathison, it needs to apply itself to the principle of modelling excellence and develop in a way that meets the societal and systemic needs and expectations of the 21st Century. I have suggested some ways that NLP may approach this:

- ❧ **Demonstrate effectiveness through empirical research studies.** Studies should include both qualitative and quantitative approaches as well as practice based evidence. Each of these hold importance rather than just the perceived gold standard of the randomised control trial. It is only by developing the softer research approaches in understanding NLP that the field can be in a position to conduct harder trials that are controlled and meet the standards required of the funders of services.

- ❧ **Supervision and mentoring of coaches and practitioners in the field.** In acting as advisor to ANLP and also being involved as an expert witness, supervisor or informal advisor to cases of perceived poor practice as complaints emerge, I have noticed that it is very rare that the individuals involved are in any form of supervision or peer review. For therapists supervision is mandatory and for coaches this is becoming the norm. It would be considered unethical in any other profession to interact with the psychological structure of another individual without first having some form of support to ensure that the practitioner was sufficiently psychologically mature to work in ways that are deemed to be safe and ethical.

- ❧ **Continuing professional development** is a core requirement of all other professions. ANLP have developed an online log to facilitate CPD. Yet there are many in the NLP field who undertake no form of CPD at all and who continue to operate from a limited mindset in their practice. Learning and insights into the workings of the mind, human relationships and human psychological development are being developed every day yet, as a profession, NLP practitioners have no core requirement to undertake CPD unless they are a member of one of the therapy organisations.

∞ Standards of training. There are still considerable variations in the standards of training for NLP programmes. It is possible to gain practitioner and master practitioner status from online or distance learning programmes where there is no requirement to work with another person, or to have the application of skills supervised or assessed. At the other end of the spectrum some NLP practitioner and master practitioner programmes are taught as year long programmes, with each programme requiring comprehensive written work and supervised practice before the person is certificated. At the most intensive level of training for UKCP accreditation, a total of 4 years of training is required in the modality with additional case work of a minimum of 450 client contact hours, personal therapy and case work supervision of 1 hour to every 6 hours of client contact time.

∞ Code of ethics and conduct. At the moment there is no compulsory requirement for NLP practitioners to operate from a code of ethics and conduct. The only exceptions are UKCP where it is considered to be core practice. Only a few training schools address ethics as part of their training and some of the anecdotal and complaints based evidence would suggest that NLP is very good at talking about the presuppositions and not as good at applying them in practice.

In any work, you are going to use words to influence the psychological life of an individual today;
you are going to use words to influence his organic life today,
you are going to use words to influence his organic life twenty years from today.

So you had better know what you are saying.

You had better be willing to reflect upon the words you use, to wonder what the meanings are,
and to seek out and understand their many associations.

Milton H. Erickson

References

Adler, A. (1927/1992). *Understanding Human Nature*. (trans. Brett. C.) Oxford: Oneworld Publications.

Agne, R.R., (2007) *Reframing practices in moral conflict: interaction problems in the negotiation standoff at Waco*. Discourse & Society, Vol. 18, No. 5, 549-578.

Allen, K. L., (1982) *An investigation of the effectiveness of Neurolinguistic Programming procedures in treating snake phobics*. Dissertation Abstracts International 43(3), 861-B University of Missouri at Kansas City.

Allen, W., (2002) *Coaching Amateur Athletes: From Frozen to Fearless*. In Grodzki, Lynn (Ed.), The new private practice: Therapist-coaches share stories, strategies, and advice. New York US: W. W. Norton & Co Inc.

Argyle M., Salter, V., Nicholson, H., Williams, M., & Burgess, P., (1970) *The Communication of Inferior and Superior Attitudes by Verbal and Non-Verbal Signals*. British Journal of Social and Clinical Psychology, v 9, pp222-231.

Bandler, R., (1992) *Magic in Action*. California: Meta Publications.

Bandler, R. & Grinder, J. (1975) *Patterns of the Hypnotic Techniques of Milton H. Erickson, M.D. Volume 1*. California: Meta Publications.

Bandler, R. & Grinder, J. (1975a) *The Structure of Magic. 1* California: Science and Behaviour Books.

Bandler, R. & Grinder, J. (1975b) *Patterns of the Hypnotic Techniques of Milton H. Erickson, M.D. Volume 1*. California: Meta Publications.

Bandler, R. & Grinder, J. (1976) *The Structure of Magic. II* California: Science and Behaviour Books.

Bandler, R. & Grinder, J. (1977) *Patterns of the Hypnotic Techniques of Milton H. Erickson, M.D. Volume 2*. California: Meta Publications.

Bandler, R. & Grinder, J. (1979) *Frogs into Princes*. Utah: Real People Press.

Bandler, R., & Grinder, J. (1983) *Reframing: Neurolinguistic Programming and the Transformation of Meaning*. Utah: Real People Press.

Bandler, R., Grinder, J., & Satir V., (1976) *Changing with Families*. California: Meta Publications.

Bandler, R. (1985) *Using Your Brain for a Change: Neurolinguistic Programming*. Utah: Real People Press.

Bandura, A. (1977) *Social Learning Theory*. Englewood Cliffs, NJ: Prentice-Hall.

Banner, S. & Wake, L. (2008) *Qualitative Studies. Neurolinguistic Programming. A blueprint for success for Keepmoat*. Rapport Magazine for ANLP. Spring 2008. Issue 11. pp.36-37.

Bateson, G. (1972/2000) *Steps to an Ecology of Mind*. London: The University of Chicago Press.

Bateson, G., Jackson, D. D., Haley, J., & Weakland, J.H. (1956) *Towards a Theory of Schizophrenia*. Behavioural Science. 1: 251-264.

Beck, D.E. & Cowan, C.C. (1996) *Spiral Dynamics: Mastering Values, Leadership and Change* Oxford: Blackwell.

Beeden, S. (2009) *Applying Dilts' 'Disney Creativity Strategy' within the Higher Education Arts, Design and Media Learning Environment*. Current Research in NLP: Volume 1 – Proceedings of 2008 Conference. Pp.96-108.

Beeman, M., Friedman, R. B., Grafman, J., Perez , E., Diamond, S., & Beadle Lindsay, M. (1994). *Summation priming and coarse semantic coding in the right hemisphere*. Journal of Cognitive Neuroscience, 6, 26-45.

Birdwhistell, R.L., (1970) *Kinesics and Context - Essays on Body-Motion Communication*. Harmondsworth: Penguin Press.

Bihrle, A. M., Brownell, H. H., & Powelson, J. A. (1986). *Comprehension of humorous and nonhumorous materials by left and right brain-damaged patients*. Brain & Cognition. 5, 399-411.

Bodenhamer, B.G. & Hall, L.M. (1999) *The Users Manual for the Brain. Volume 1* Bancyfelin: Crown House Publishing.

Bostic St. Clair, C., & Grinder, J. (2001). *Whispering In The Wind*. Scotts Valley, California: J & C En2 Bantam Books.

Churches, R. & Terry, R., (2007) *NLP for Teachers: How to be a Highly Effective Teacher.* Carmarthen: Crown House Publishing.

Churches, R., & West-Burnham, J. (2009) *Leading Learning Through Relationships The Implications of Neuro-linguistic Programming for Personalisation and the Children's Agenda in England.* Current Research in NLP Volume – Proceedings of 2008 Conference pp.6-20.

Clark, L. (2008) *Clinical Leadership: Values, Beliefs and Vision.* Nursing Management 15 (7). pp.30-35.

Coalter, M. (2008) *How I Made a Difference at Work.* People Management. 29.5.2008 (1358 – 6297).

Cowan, N. (2001) *The Magical Number 4 in Short-Term Memory: A Reconsideration of Mental Storage Capacity.* Behavioral and Brain Sciences. 24 (1) 87-185.

Curreen, M.P. (1995) *A Simple Hypnotically Based NLP Technique used with two Clients in a Criminal Justice Setting.* Australian Journal of Clinical and Experimental Hypnosis. 23 (1) pp. 51-57.

Damasio, A. (1994) *Descartes Error. Emotion, Reason and the Human Brain.* New York: Penguin.

Davis, G. L., (1984) *Neurolinguistic Programming as an interviewing technique with prelingually deaf adults.* Dissertation Abstracts International 46(5), 1247-A (1248-A) Oklahoma State University.

Day, R. C. G., *Students' Perceptions of Neurolinguistic Programming Strategies (counseling, communication, clients, therapy).* Dissertation Abstracts International 46(4), 1333-B Florida State University.

DeLozier, J. (1985) *Mastery, New Coding and Systemic NLP.* NLP World. Vol 2. 1.

Diamantopoulos, G., Wooley, S.I., & Spann, M., (2009) *A Critical Review of Past Research into the Neuro-linguistic Programming Eye-Accessing Cues Model.* Current Research in NLP Volume – Proceedings of 2008 Conference pp.6-20.

Dilts, R., & Grinder J., (1989) *Neurolinguistic Programming: The Study of the Structure of Subjective Experience. Volume I.* California: Meta Publications.

Dilts, R., Grinder, J., Bandler, R., & DeLozier, J. (1980) *Neurolnguistic Programming:Volume 1, the Study of the Structure of Subjective Experience.* California: Meta Publications.

Dilts, R. (1990) *Changing Belief Systems with NLP.* California: Meta Publications.

Dilts, R., (1994) *Strategies of Genius. Volume 1.* California: Meta Publications.

Dilts, R. (1999) *Sleight of Mouth. The Magic of Conversational Belief Change.* California: Metapublications.

Doemland, J. (2001) *Language and Performance: An NLP Meta-Model Analysis of Performance Descriptions by Elite Canoe-Slalom Athletes.* Dissertation Abstracts International, B: Sciences and Engineering, 61 (10) Apr, 5267-B.

Duch, W., Matykiewicz, P., & Pestian, J., (2008). *Neurolinguistic Approach to Natural Language Processing with Applications to Medical Text Analysis.* Neural Networks. 21 (10) pp. 1500.

Einspruch, E.L., & Forman, B.D., (1985) *Observations Concerning Research Literature on Neuro-Linguistic Programming,* in Journal of Counselling Psychology, 32:4, 589-596.

Einspruch, E.L., & Forman, B.D. (1988) *Neurolinguistic Programming in the Treatment of Phobias.* Psychotherapy in Private Practice. 6:1, 91-100.

Erickson, M.H., Rossi, E.L, & Rossi, S.I. (1976/2001) Milton H. Erickson's *Approach to Trance Induction.* Paper presented to the Society for Clinical and Experimental Hypnosis, in Milton H. Erickson M.D.: The Complete Works. (Digital media published by the Milton H. Erickson Foundation).

Erickson, M. H. & Rossi, E.L. (1989) *The February Man. Evolving Consciousness and Identity in Hypnotherapy.* New York: Brunner Mazel.

Erickson, M. H. (1985). (Eds. Rossi, E. L. & Ryan, M. *The Lectures, Seminars and Workshops of Milton H. Erickson. Vol II. Life Reframing in Hypnosis.* New York: Irvington.

European Association for Neurolinguistic Programming (EANLP), (2010). Available online. Accessed 12.10.2010. http://www.eanlpt.org/

Ferguson, D. M., (1987) *The effect of two audiotaped Neurolinguistic Programming (NLP) phobia treatments on public speaking anxiety.* Dissertation Abstracts International .

Field, E.S., (1990) *Neurolinguistic Programming as an Adjunct to other Psychotherapeutic/hypnotherapeutic Interventions.* The American Journal of clinical hypnosis 32 (3) pp.174-182.

Forman, B.D. (1986) *Neuro-Linguistic Programming in Couple Therapy* Paper presented at the Annual Conference of the American Association for Marriage and Family Therapy (44th, Orlando, FL, October 23-26, 1986). pp. 11.

Fremder, L. A. (1986) *Generalization of Visual Dot Pattern Strategies to Number Pattern Strategies by Learning Disabled Students.* Dissertation Abstracts International 47(11), 4055-A Columbia University Teachers College.

Freud, S. (1904). Freud's *Psycho-analytic Procedure.* In J. Strachley (Ed & Trans). Standard Edition of the Complete Psychological Works of Sigmund Freud. Vol. 7. London: Hogarth Press.

Gallese, V. (2001) *The 'shared manifold' hypothesis. From mirror neurons to empathy.* Journal of Consciousness Studies. 85(5-7), pp.33-50.

Gallese, V., & Goldman, A., (1998) *Mirror neurons and the simulation theory of mind reading.* Trends in Cognitive Sciences. 2 pp. 493-501.

Gallese, V., Fadiga, L., Fogassi, L., & Rizzolatti, G. (1996) *Action recognition in the pre-motor cortex.* Brain. 119. pp.593-609.

Gallese, V. 2007) *Intentional Attunement: Mirror Neurons and the Neural Underpinnings of Interpersonal Relations.* Journal of the American Psychoanalytic Association. 55 (1) pp. 131-175.

Gawler-Wright, P. (1999) *The Skills of Love.* London: BeeLeaf Publishing.

Gawler-Wright, P. (2004) *Intermediate Contemporary Psychotherapy Volume 1* London:BeeLeaf Publishing.

Gawler-Wright, P. (2006 edition) *Wider Mind; Ericksonian Psychotherapy in Practice* London:BeeLeaf Publishing.

Gawler-Wright, P. (2007 edition) *Intermediate Contemporary Psychotherapy Volume 2, 2007 Edition* London: BeeLeaf Publishing.

Genser-Medlitsch, M., & Schütz, P. (1997) *Does Neuro-Linguistic psychotherapy have effect? New Results shown in the extramural section.* Austria:EANLP.

Gerhardt, S. (2004) *Why Love Matters. How Affection Shapes a Baby's Brain.* London: Routledge.

Glaser, D. E., Grezes, J.S., Calvo, B., Passingham, R.E., Haggard. P., (2004) *Functional Imaging of Motor Experience and Expertise During Action Observation.* University College, London.

Gordon, D., (1978/1989) *Therapeutic Metaphors: Helping Others Through the Looking Glass.* California: Metapublications.

Graves, C.W., Huntley, W.C., LaBier, D.W. (1965) *Personality Structure and Perceptual Readiness. An Investigation of Their Relationship to Hypothesized Levels of Human Existence.* Union College. Document available online: <http://www.claregraves.com/articles-content/1965_GHL/1965_GHL1.html>

Gray, R. (2009) *The Brooklyn Program: Applying NLP to Addictions.* Current Research in NLP: Volume 1. Proceedings of 2008 Conference pp.84-94.

Gray, R. (2010) PTSD: *Extinction, Reconsolidation and the Visual-Kinesthetic Dissociation Protocol.* Traumatology.

Grinder, J., Bandler, R., Andreas, C., (1981) *Tranceformations: Neurolinguistic Programming and the Structure of Hypnosis.* Utah: Real People Press.

Grinder, J., & DeLozier, J. (1987) *Turtles all the Way Down.* Portland, Oregon: Metamorphous press.

Hale, R. L., (1986) *The effects of Neurolinguistic Programming (NLP) on public speaking anxiety and incompetence.* Dissertation Abstracts International 47(5).

Hall, L.M. (1995/2000) *Meta-States: Managing the Higher Levels of Your Mind's Reflexivity.* Clifton, Colorado: Neuro-Semantics Publications.

Henwood, S., & Lister, J. (2007) *NLP and Coaching for Health Care Professionals: Developing Expert Practice.* Oxford: Wiley.

Hirst, W., LeDoux, J., & Stein, S. (1984). *Constraints on the Processing of Indirect Speech Acts: Evidence from Aphasiology.* Brain & Language. 23, 26-33.

Hossack, A., & Standidge, K. (1993) *Using an imaginary scrapbook for neurolinguistic programming in the aftermath of a clinical depression: a case history.* Gerontologist. 33(2):265-8.

James, T. & Woodsmall, W. (1988) *Time Line Therapy and the Basis of Personality.* California: Metapublications.

James. W. (1884). *What is an Emotion?* Mind 9, 188-205.

Jung, C.G. (1921/1971) *Psychological Types* London:Routledge & Kegan Paul.

Jung. C.G. (1964) *Man and his Symbols.* London: Aldus Books Ltd.

Kammer, D., Lanver, C., Schwochow, M., (1997) *Controlled treatment of simple phobias with NLP: evaluation of a pilot project.* University of Bielefeld, Department of Psychology, unpublished paper.

Kayes, D.C. (2005) *Internal Validity and Reliability of Kolb's Learning Style Inventory Version 3 (1999)* Journal of Business and Psychology. 20 (2) pp. 249-257.

Kazmerski, V. A., Blasko, D.G., & Banchiamlack, G.D. (2003) *ERP and Behavioural Evidence of Individual Differences in Metaphor Comprehension.* Memory and Cognition. 31 (5) pp.673-689.

Klein, M. (1932) *The Psychoanalysis of Children.* London: Hogarth.

Kolb, D. A., Rubin, I. M., & McIntyre, J. (Eds., 1971). *Organizational Psychology: An Experiential Approach.* Englewood Cliffs, NJ: Prentice Hall.

Koob, J.J., & Funk J. (2002) *Kolb's Learning Style Inventory: Issues of Reliability and Validity.* Research on Social Work Practice. 12 (2) pp. 293.

Korzybski, A.O. (1933/1948) *Science and Sanity.* Institute of General Semantics.

Kostere, K. & Malatesta, L. (1990) *Maps, Models and the Structure of Reality. NLP technology in Psychotherapy.* Portland, Oregon: Metamorphous press.

Koziey, P. W.; McLeod, G., (1987) *Visual-Kinesthetic Dissociation in Treatment of Victims of Rape (Research and Practice)* Professional Psychology: Research and Practice. American Psychological Association.

Krugman, M., Kirsch, I., Wickless, C., Milling, L., Golicz, H., Toth, A., (1985) *Neuro-Linguistic Programming Treatment for Anxiety: Magic or Myth?* Journal of Consulting & Clinical Psychology. 53(4):526-530.

Lawley, J. & Tomkins, P. (2005) *Metaphors in Mind. Transformation through Symbolic Modelling* UK: The Developing Company Press.

Lazarus, J. (2006) *Ahead of the Game. How to Use Your Mind to Win in Sport.* Cornwall: Ecadamy Press.

Liberman, M. B., (1984) *The treatment of simple phobias with Neurolinguistic Programming techniques.* Dissertation Abstracts International 45(6), St. Louis University.

Linder-Pelz, S., (2008) *Meta-coaching: a methodology grounded in psychological theory* International Journal of Evidence Based Coaching and Mentoring Vol. 6, No.1, Pp 43.

Linder-Pelz, S. (2010) *NLP Coaching. An Evidence-Based Approach for Coaches, Leaders and Individuals.* London: Kogan Page.

Locke. E.A., (1968) *Toward a Theory of Task Motivation and Incentives.* Organisational Behaviour and Human Performance. Vol 3 (2), 157-189.

Locke, E.A. & Latham, G.P. (1990) *A Theory of Goal Setting and Task Performance* Englewood Cliffs, NJ: Prentice Hall.

Lorenz, K. (1935) *Der Kumpan in der Umwelt des Vogels. Der Artgenosse als auslösendes moment sozialer verhaltensweisen* Journal für ornithologie 83:137-215, 289-413.

Lorenz, K. (1970) *Studies in animal and human behaviour. Volume 1* Cambridge MA: Harvard University Press.

Malloy, T. E., Mitchell, C., Gordon, O. E,. (1987) *Training Cognitive Strategies underlying Intelligent Problem Solving.* Perceptual and Motor Skills 64: 1039-1046.

Maslow, A. (1943). *A Theory of Human Motivation.* Psychological Review, 50. 370-96. Washington DC: American Psychology Association.

Massey, M. (1979) *People Puzzle: Understanding Yourself and Others.* Virginia Reston Publishing Co.

McCarthy, B. (1987) *The 4Mat Workbook: Guided Practice in 4Mat Lesson and Unit Planning.* Illinois: About Learning Inc.

McDermott, I. & Jago, W (2001) *Brief NLP Therapy* London: Sage Publications.

Mehrabian, A., & Wiener, M., (1967a) *Decoding of Inconsistent Communications.* Journal of Personality and Social Psychology, Vol. 6, No. 1, May 1967, pp. 109-114.

Mehrabian, A., & Ferris, S. R., (1967b) *Inference of Attitudes from Nonverbal Communication in Two Channels* Journal of Consulting Psychology, Vol. 31, No. 3, pp. 248-258.

Mehrabian, A. (1971). *Silent messages: Implicit communication of emotions and attitudes*. Belmont, CA: Wadsworth.

Miller, G. 1956) *The Magical Number Seven, Plus or Minus Two: Some Limits on Our Capacity for Processing Information*. Princeton University : Psychological Review.

Miller, G., Galanter, E. & Pribram, K. (1960) *Plans and the Structure of Behaviour*. New York: Holt, Rinehart and Wilson.

Murata, M., Uchimoto, K., Ma, Q., Isahara, J, (2001) *Magical Number Seven Plus or Minus Two: Syntactic Structure Recognition in Japanese and English Sentences*. in Lecture Notes in Computer Science. Computational Linguistics and Intelligent Text Processing (2009) Heidelberg: Springer Berlin.

Myers, I. (1962) *The Myers-Briggs Type Indicator*. Palo Alto: Consulting Psychologists Press.

Neurolinguistic Psychotherapy and Counselling Association. (2010) Available online. Accessed 12.01.2010. www.nlptca.org

O'Connor, J. (2001) *NLP Workbook*. London: Harper Collins Publishers Ltd.

O'Connor, J. & Seymour, J. (1990) *Introducing NLP. Psychological Skills for Understanding and Influencing People*. London: Thorsons.

Ordóñez, L.D., Schweitzer, M.E., Galinsky, A.D., & Bazerman, M.H., (2009) *On Good Scholarship, Goal Setting, and Scholars Gone Wild*. Academy of Management Perspectives. 23 (3), 82-87.

Oxford English Dictionary. www.askoxford.com Available online. Accessed 15 February 2010.

Pareto, V.F.D. (1935) *Mind and Society* 3. Montana: Kessinger Publishing.

Parnes., S. J. (1992) *Source Book for Creative Problem Solving*. Buffalo: Creative Foundation Press.

Pavlov, I.P. (1927) *Conditioned Reflexes*. London: Routledge (Original work published 1904).

Perls, F., Hefferline, F. & Goodman, P. (1951/1973) *Gestalt Therapy. Excitement & Growth in the Human Personality*. New York: Julian Press Dell Publishing.

Perls, F.S. (1969) *Ego, Hunger and Aggression*. The Beginning on Gestalt Therapy. New York: Vintage Books.

Pert, C. (1997) *Molecules of Emotion. Why You Feel the Way You Feel*. London: Pocket Books.

Prochaska, J.L. & DiClemente, C.C. (1992) (Hersen, M.: Eisler, R., & Miller, P.M., Eds) *Stages of change in the modification of problem behaviour. Progress in behaviour modification* 28. Sycamore, IL: Sycamore Publishing Company.

Ramachandran. V.S., (accessed on line 11/08/09) *Mirror Neurons and Imitation Learning as the Driving Force behind 'The Great Leap Forward' in Human Evolution* http://www.edge.org/3rd_culture/ramachandran/ramachandran_p1.html

Ramachandran. V.S., Depalma, N., Lisiewski, S. (2009) *The Role of Mirror Neurons in Processing Vocal Emotions: Evidence from Psychophysiological Data*. International Journal of Neuroscinece. 119 (5). Pp.681-691 (11).

Rapp. A.M., Leube, D.T., Erb, M., Grodd, W., & Tilo, T.J.K (2006) *Laterality in Metaphor Processing: Lack of Evidence from Functional Magnetic Resonance Imaging for the Right Hemisphere Theory*. Dept of Psychiatry, University of Tuebingen, Germany.

Rizzolatti, G., Fadiga. L., Fogassi, L., & Gallese, V. (1999) *Resonance Behaviours and Mirror Neurons*. Archives of Italian Biology. 137 pp. 85-100.

Robbins, A. (1991) *Awaken the Giant Within*. New York Fireside.

Rosen, S. (1992) *My Voice will go with you. The Teaching Tales of Milton H. Erickson*. New York:W.W. Norton & Company.

Sandhu, D. S., (1991) *Application of Neurolinguistic Programming for Treatment and Relapse Prevention of Addictive Behaviors*. Paper presented at the Annual Convention of the American Association for Counseling and Development (Reno, NV, April 21-24, 1991). pp. 31.

Sandhu, D. S., et al (1991) *Cross-Cultural Counselling and Neurolinguistic Mirroring: An Exploration of Empathy, Trustworthiness, and Positive Interaction with Native American Adolescents*. Paper presented at the Annual Meeting of the American Association for Counseling and Development (Baltimore, MD, March 27-30, 1992). , pp. 26.

Satir, V. (1972) *Peoplemaking*. Palo Alto: Science and Behaviour Books.

Schore, A.N. (2003) *Affect Regulation and the Repair of the Self.* London: W.W. Norton.

Shannon, C.E., & Weaver, W., (1949) *A Mathematical Model of Communication.* Urbana, IL: University of Illinois Press .

Short, D., Erickson, B.A., Erickson Klein, R., (2005) *Hope and Resiliency: Understanding the Psychotherapeutic Strategies of Milton H. Erickson.* Carmarthen Wales, Crown House.

Simpkins, C.A., Simpkins, A.M., (2008) *An Exploratory Outcome Comparison between an Ericksonian Approach to Therapy and Brief Dynamic Therapy.* American Journal of Clinical Hypnosis. 50 (3) 217-32.

Skinner, B.F. (1938) *The Behaviour of Organisms* New York: Appleton-Century-Crofts.

Skinner, B.F. (1961) *Teaching Machines.* Scientific American: 205(5): 90-107.

Skinner, H., & Stephens, P. (2003) *Speaking the Same Language: the Relevance of Neurolinguistic Programming to Effective Marketing Communications.* Journal of Marketing Communications. 9 (3) pp. 177-192.

Solms, M., (1996) *Towards an anatomy of the unconscious.* Journal of Clinical Psychoanalysis. 5. pp.331-367.

Sparrow. S., (2006) *Get with the Programme.* Personnel Today. 20/6/06.

Squirrel. L., (2009) *Can Neuro-Linguistic Programming work with Young Children who display varying Social, Emotional and Behavioural Difficulties?* Current Research in NLP: Volume 1. Proceedings of 2008 Conference pp.109-120.

Sterman, C.M. (1990) *Neurolinguistic Programming in Alcoholism Treatment.* Binghamton, New York: The Haworth Press.

Stern, D. (1985) *The Interpersonal World of the Infant.* New York: Basic Books.

Stern, N. (1998) *The Motherhood Constellation. A Unified View of Parent-Infant Psychotherapy.* London: Karnac Books.

Stern, D. (1995) *The Infant In Us All: A Review of The Motherhood Constellation: A Unified View of Parent-Infant Psychotherapy.* New York: Basic Books.

Sullivan, W., Sullivan, R., Buffton, B., (2001) *Aligning Individual and Organisational Values to Support Change.* Journal of Change Management. 2 (3) pp. 247-254.

Swets, J. A., & Bjork, R. A., (1990) *Enhancing Human Performance: An Evaluation of "New Age" Techniques considered by the U.S. Army.* Psychological Science 1(2): 85-86,

Titone, D. (1998). *Hemispheric differences in context sensitivity during lexical ambiguity resolution.* Brain & Language, 65, 361-394.

Tosey, P., & Mathison, J., (2009) *Neuro-Linguistic Programming: A Critical Appreciation for Managers and Developers.* Basingstoke: Palgrave Macmillan.

Tubbs, M.E. (1986) *Goal Setting: A Meta-analytic Examination of the Empirical Evidence.* Journal of Applied Psychology. Vol 71 (3) 474-483.

Turan, B., & Townsley Stemberger, R.M., (2000) *The Effectiveness of Matching Language to Enhance Perceived Empathy.* Communication and Cognition 33 (3-4) pp. 287-300.

Twitmeyer, E.B. (1902) *A Study of the Knee-Jerk.* Unpublished doctorial dissertation, University of Pennsylvania.

Wake, L. (2008) *Neurolinguistic Psychotherapy: A Postmodern Approach.* London: Routledge.

Wales, S. (2002) *Why Coaching?* Journal of Change Management. 3 (3) pp275-282.

Walker, L. (2004) *Changing with NLP: A Casebook of Neuro-Linguistic Programming in Medical Practice.* Oxford: Radcliffe Medical Press.

Walton, M., Adams, I., McCarthy, M., (2009) T*he Experience of Regular Participation for Women Moving into their Middle Years: its Nature, Meaning and its benefits.* Current Research in NLP: Volume 1. Proceedings of 2008 Conference pp.21-32.

Watson, J.B., Rayner, R. (1920) *Conditioned Emotional Reactions.* Journal of Experimental Psychology, 3, 1-14.

Watzlawick, P. (1978) *The Language of Change. Elements of Therapeutic Communication.* New York: W.W. Norton & Company.

Weaver, M. (2009) *An Exploration of a Research-Based Approach to the Evaluation of Clients' Experience of Neuro-Linguistic Psychotherapy within a Private Practice Making use of the CORE Model.* Current Research in NLP: Proceedings of 2008 NLP Conference. Vol 1. pp67- 83.

Wiener, N., (1948) *Cybernetics or Control and Communication in the Animal and the Machine.* Cambridge, MA: MIT Press.

Winner, E., & Gardner, H. (1977). *The comprehension of metaphor in brain-damaged patients.* Brain, 100, 717-729.

Woodsmall. W *The Science of Advanced Behavioural Modelling.* International Research Institute for Human Typological Studies, USA.

Young, J. A., (1995) *Developing Leadership from within: A Descriptive Study of the use of Neurolinguistic Programming Practices in a Course on Leadership.* The Ohio State University, US Dissertation Abstract Dissertation Abstracts International Section A: Humanities and Social Sciences. Vol 56(1-A), pp. 0080.

NLP: Principles in Practice

1305263R0

Printed in Great Britain by
Amazon.co.uk, Ltd.,
Marston Gate.